IRANIAN NUCLEAR TALKS: NEGOTIATING A BAD DEAL?

HEARING

BEFORE THE

SUBCOMMITTEE ON TERRORISM, NONPROLIFERATION, AND TRADE

OF THE

COMMITTEE ON FOREIGN AFFAIRS HOUSE OF REPRESENTATIVES

ONE HUNDRED THIRTEENTH CONGRESS

SECOND SESSION

NOVEMBER 18, 2014

Serial No. 113–227

Printed for the use of the Committee on Foreign Affairs

Available via the World Wide Web: http://www.foreignaffairs.house.gov/ or http://www.gpo.gov/fdsys/

U.S. GOVERNMENT PRINTING OFFICE

91–453PDF WASHINGTON : 2014

For sale by the Superintendent of Documents, U.S. Government Printing Office
Internet: bookstore.gpo.gov Phone: toll free (866) 512–1800; DC area (202) 512–1800
Fax: (202) 512–2104 Mail: Stop IDCC, Washington, DC 20402–0001

(II)

CONTENTS

IRANIAN NUCLEAR TALKS: NEGOTIATING A BAD DEAL?

TUESDAY, NOVEMBER 18, 2014

House of Representatives,
Subcommittee on Terrorism, Nonproliferation, and Trade,
Committee on Foreign Affairs,
Washington, DC.

The committee met, pursuant to notice, at 2 o'clock p.m., in room 2200 Rayburn House Office Building, Hon. Ted Poe (chairman of the subcommittee) presiding.

Mr. POE. Subcommittee will come to order. Without objection, all members may have 5 days to submit statements, questions and extraneous materials for the record subject to the length limitation in the rules.

If someone could get the back door, it would be appreciated. It is not to keep you in or keep anyone out. We just want the door shut.

Iran has defied and lied to the international community for over a decade when it comes to its nuclear weapons program. Finally, the West got serious and took a stand and imposed real sanctions in 2012.

The sanctions actually worked and Iran came to the negotiating table, but then the West retreated. Loosening up on sanctions just when Iran was beginning to feel the consequences of its actions was a monumental mistake.

Netanyahu was correct. When this deal was made by the Secretary of State he said that this was a bad deal, a very bad deal for Israel and for the United States and for world safety. Since then, Iranian leaders have been emboldened by the economic relief they have experienced and they have reverted to their defiant ways.

Recently, a top advisor to Iranian President Hassan Rouhani said, "Obama is the weakest of all U.S. Presidents." Now is the time for the leader of the free world to prove Iran wrong.

The world, including our enemies and allies, are watching. We have already passed the deadline for negotiations to end in July and now we await a second deadline, which is next week. There is reason to believe that the Iranians——[Loses sound.]

After all, we will continue to pay them millions whether the deadline is met or not, just for the promise of cooperation—a promise from, really, an enemy of the world. Each attempt at compromise has turned out to be a stall tactic by the Iranians.

(1)

While the Iranians have their first string varsity team, we are playing our JV team, to quote a phrase. As it is, we don't know how many centrifuges the Iranians currently have. The old principle of trust but verify does not work in this case because Iran has shown that it cannot be trusted.

They will lie when the truth is not in their political interest. The IAEA hasn't been able to verify Iran's capabilities. The Iranians could have a bomb in as little as 3 months.

The problem is we don't know and neither does the IAEA. Making matters worse, we can't take the Iranians at their word on their nuclear aspirations. They still haven't come clean about their previous suspected nuclear weapons activities alleged by the IAEA back in November 2011.

Iran's real aspirations are simple. They want to annihilate Israel, and then they want to annihilate the United States. That is what the real leader of Iran, Khamenei, called for just last week.

We are dealing with the devil and the clock is running out. The deal cannot be handled solely behind doors away from the public and away from scrutiny. There are dire consequences in these negotiations and the American people expect their representatives—the U.S. Congress—to play a role.

The U.S. Congress must approve or disapprove any potential final nuclear agreement with Iran. Here is what an acceptable agreement might look like.

One, Iran would verifiably take apart its illicit nuclear infrastructure; two, Iran would resolve all past issues of concern including possible military aspects of its nuclear program development; three, the inspections regime must go beyond the authorities that the IAEA currently has; four, a permanent inspections team in Iran is needed and they must be allowed to go anywhere, see anything at any time; five, Iran must come into compliance with all six standing U.N. Security Council resolutions related to its nuclear program; and six, Iran's ballistic missiles program must be addressed.

Missiles, after all, can be used to deliver nuclear weapons. Any deal that does not address this is not only a bad deal but a dangerous one. We have to address the issue of deliveries.

And seven, finally, no sanctions relief should be provided unless a final agreement can verify and permanently prevent Iran from acquiring nuclear weapons.

Even if an acceptable agreement is reached, the sanctions relief must be limited and phased so that we can keep our economic leverage. In general, any good agreement is not about freezing Iran's nuclear program but dismantling it. Anything less simply postpones the inevitable danger that a nuclear-armed Iran presents to the world.

I look forward to hearing what our witnesses think about where we are and what we should be doing in Congress. The U.S. must be clear and unequivocal. There will be no reductions in sanctions without verified steps to show that Tehran is abandoning, not just freezing, its nuclear weapons program.

I will now yield to the ranking member, Mr. Sherman from California, for his opening statement.

Mr. SHERMAN. Thank you, Chairman Poe, for holding these important hearings.

I agree with you that any sanctions relief should come only through an act of Congress and I hope that the Iranians understand that any waivers granted by this President are waivers that do not necessarily apply to any future administration.

Furthermore, looking at the statute, waivers are supposed to be case by case based upon the entity applying for the waiver, not blanket waivers in effect suspending our sanctions statutes.

The one possible disagreement I have with you is I don't think that even at their high water mark our sanctions were enough to really bring Iran to the table if that is the table where they are supposed to give up their nuclear program.

We had sanctions significant enough to get them to come to the table where they do a kabuki dance and get some relief from the sanctions because it is always better to help your economy at least even from modest sanctions.

So to say that we ever had sanctions significant enough to threaten regime survival and to cause this regime to be willing to give up its nuclear weapons program is questionable.

The Joint Plan of Action gave Iran some very significant relief. First, it caused a pause in the reductions of oil purchases that were called for by the Menendez-Kirk provisions of the 2012 law.

Second, it stopped Congress cold from adopting new sanctions statutes. And finally, and perhaps most importantly, it changed the whole psychology, and much of economics is psychology. It caused people interested in the Iranian economy to think that things would be on the upswing. Under this Joint Plan of Action, we are giving Iran $700 million, albeit of its own money, every month.

I think we have got to be loud and clear to the administration that further releases of Iran's frozen funds should not occur just because we are going into a new month. If these talks are extended they shouldn't be extended with us paying a price for that extension.

Now, we are in a much weaker bargaining position than we were at the beginning of this century. During the first decade of this century, we didn't enforce our sanctions laws.

The administration worked very effectively and successfully to prevent us from passing any new sanctions laws and the Shiites were put in control of Iraq. So today, we have to deal with a much weaker hand than if we had started to take this program seriously at the beginning of the century.

We are told that this JPOA has frozen Iran's program. That is not true and, to some extent, is true. Some of the program has been frozen. Some of it has been rolled back, particularly the 20 percent enriched uranium.

Half has been diluted. Another half has been oxidized. But keep in mind even that oxidized portion is far more than Iran needs for any peaceful purpose. It is oxidized but it hasn't been converted into fuel, pellets or rods so it is pretty available for use in creating a bomb and it is more than a bomb's worth.

So, even under this JPOA, they are close to their first nuclear weapon. But what concerns me just as much is their centrifuges are still turning, creating more and more low-enriched uranium that is oxidized, but reversing that oxidization process is rather easy, low technology and quick.

This committee has been assured by the administration that, as part of this deal, we would learn of the possible military dimensions, or PMDs, of the Iranian program.

Iran has stonewalled the IAEA on that and it should be part of any reduction of sanctions or any continuation of the suspension of Kirk-Menendez that we find out and that the IAEA is given answers to its questions.

On the other hand, the JPOA has pretty much frozen the Arak plutonium reactor and that is one of its positive elements. In looking at a final agreement, a lot of focus is on how long the agreement will last, what enrichment will be allowed and how that enrichment will be monitored.

We need to look just as much at how much uranium and in what enrichment levels Iran is able to stockpile and what tracing of ore and monitoring of ore and yellow cake is there so that we can make sure that the total grams of enriched uranium both in terms of quantity and enrichment level is consistent with the allegedly peaceful nature of Iran's program.

Finally, I am going to be asking our witnesses to help us identify how we can draft strong sanctions legislation that will go into effect in a few months unless Congress receives and approves a good deal negotiated with Iran.

As I said, these sanctions would have to be regime threatening. They would have to go beyond where we were before these negotiations began, and I look forward to working with all of the members of this subcommittee and our witnesses to make sure that we are ready with sanctions that will go into effect early next year unless Iran enters into a good deal with the United States.

I say that not to make our negotiators' position more difficult but because only with such strong sanctions legislation is there any hope that they will be successful. I yield back.

Mr. POE. The Chair will recognize other members for their 1-minute opening statements. The Chair recognizes the gentleman from South Carolina, Mr. Wilson, for a minute.

Mr. WILSON. Thank you, Mr. Chairman. Mr. Chairman, I thank you for your leadership, and Ranking Member Sherman. It is really reassuring to see Members of Congress working together facing a common threat. This is so unusual.

I am just so pleased to see you working together and all of us working together, hopefully, on this subcommittee. I agree very much with the senior senator of South Carolina, Lindsey Graham, who, this weekend, pointed out that the administration needs to understand that this Iranian regime cares more about trying to weaken America and push us out of the Middle East than cooperating with us.

Until we recognize that reality and formulate a regional strategy to counter the Iranian regime's malign influence, we will continue to harm U.S. national security interest. Additionally, I support holding the President accountable by requiring congressional approval of any deal that is reached with Iran, and I want to conclude by agreeing with Prime Minister Benjamin Netanyahu who indicated, ''Iran is not your ally.''

As the Prime Minister said on Face the Nation, "Iran is not your friend. Iran is your enemy. It is not your partner. Iran is committed to the destruction of Israel."

Facing this, again, I want to thank the leadership who are here today and in a bipartisan manner to protect the people of the Middle East and the United States. Thank you.

Mr. POE. The Chair recognizes the gentleman from Illinois, Mr. Kinzinger, for 1 minute.

Mr. KINZINGER. Thank you, Mr. Chairman. I think it is important to remind everybody here that during the time of the Iraq war it is estimated that upwards of half of the Americans that were killed were killed either directly or indirectly by Iranian EFPs—explosive foreign penetrators—Iranian direct military action and things along that line.

So yeah, you are right, Mr. Wilson. They are not our friend. I think the message to Iran is simple—just stop or pay a price, and I think we had them at that position a year ago, and for some reason we saw an administration collapse in a desperate desire to enter a deal.

We knew that, of course, the first 6 months wouldn't happen so we extended another 6 months and I believe that in a week they are going to come in front of Congress and say, we need an additional 6 months, which I think would be the wrong message.

So the question here is, with the collapse of U.S. foreign policy in the last couple years, what leverage do we have and I think it is important for us, and I appreciate the chairman calling this hearing, to stand together and say that we will not allow a bad deal with Iran.

Mr. POE. I thank the gentleman. The Chair will yield 1 minute to Mr. Perry from Pennsylvania.

Mr. PERRY. Thank you, Mr. Chairman. I have, like many of us, numerous concerns regarding the Joint Plan of Action and the continued negotiations as being a viable avenue for preventing—I just stress preventing—Iran from obtaining a nuclear weapon, which is and should be the primary objective of our policy and our actions.

However, a great concern that seems to be sometimes getting lost in the more technical debate is the potential for a nuclear agreement to recognize Iran's right to enrich, and I take great exception with this.

It sets a unacceptable precedent, in my mind. Other signatory states to the Non-proliferation Treaty—the NPT—may then choose to enrich themselves after they observe Iran being allowed to continue to enrich despite breaking its NPT commitments.

A nuclear arms race is absolutely the last thing we need in this region of the world, and I yield back.

Mr. POE. The gentleman yields back his time.

The Chair will recognize the other gentleman from Illinois, Mr. Schneider, for his opening statement.

Mr. SCHNEIDER. Thank you, Mr. Chairman, and I want to thank the witnesses for joining us today on a most crucial issue as we sit less than 1 week from the deadline for negotiations under the Joint Plan of Action.

The prospect of a nuclear Iran—I believe is the single greatest threat to the region, to the world, and it is imperative that we find a way to prevent that.

If there is to be a deal it must absolutely ensure that any and all paths for Iran to get a nuclear weapon are blocked and, ultimately, permanently closed.

What I am looking forward to hearing from you all in the time we have together today is your sense of the potential for a deal, whether it is in the next week or shortly thereafter, what are the consequences and concerns if there is to be a delay further than on November 24th, as the current deadline is, and, on the assumption that there is not a deal to be had, what would be the next steps you would want to see from this Congress.

And with that, I yield back. Thank you.

Mr. POE. Do any other members wish to make an opening statement? Seeing no show of hands, the witnesses will be introduced and then they will have their time for opening statements and then proceed to questions.

Dr. Ray Takeyh is a senior fellow for Middle East studies at the Council of Foreign Relations and an adjunct professor at Georgetown University. Dr. Takeyh was previously a senior advisor on Iran at the Department of State and is widely published.

Our next witness, Mr. Matthew McInnis, is a resident fellow at the American Enterprise Institute, focusing on Iran. Previously, Mr. McInnis worked on Middle East and counterproliferation issues during his long tenure at the Defense Intelligence Agency.

And Mr. David Albright is the founder and president of the Institute for Science and International Security. Mr. Albright holds Masters degrees in both physics and mathematics.

Our first witness, Dr. Takeyh, we will start with you. You have 5 minutes. Thank you.

STATEMENT OF RAY TAKEYH, PH.D., SENIOR FELLOW FOR MIDDLE EASTERN STUDIES, COUNCIL ON FOREIGN RELATIONS

Mr. TAKEYH. Thank you, Mr. Chairman, for inviting me here. I will be brief and it is always good to be with

Mr. POE. If your mike is working.

Mr. TAKEYH. Oh, sorry. Better?

Mr. POE. A little better.

Mr. TAKEYH. I think it is fair to say—I am sure there will be agreement on this issue, perhaps even a unanimous one—that the Islamic Republic has not been responsible stakeholders in international affairs.

I don't think I am being too provocative with that. Yet, I think Iran over the years has had some success in conditioning the narrative of the nuclear negotiations.

The Iranian regime has obtained an acknowledgment of its right to enrich. That is not necessarily a right in principle but acknowledgment in practice, which is a distinction of a rather limited nature.

It has also persistently suggested that all U.N. Security Council resolutions are politically contrived and have neither authority nor legitimacy, and there may be indication that the P5+1 countries—

the five members of the Security Council and Germany—that are negotiating on this issue may actually not adhere to certain aspects of the U.N. Security Council resolution themselves, particularly the provision demanding suspension, and it is probably unlikely that a final agreement will have a suspension component and that brings into question, of course, the legitimacy of international law in this particular respect.

Iran has continued to insist that its existing enrichment capacity has to be respected and it has also maintained that any inspection modality has to be limited to the existing NPT measures which, perhaps, fall short of some of the expectations that we have.

Another aspect of the Iranian diplomacy over the past year that has been successful has been President Rouhani's notion that he has inculcated rather effectively that he is under hard pressure from hardliners at home and the implication of that being that if the Western powers want a deal they should essentially deal with him and make the necessary concessions to obtain that deal.

I don't think that is true. I think a more careful examination reveals that the Islamic Republic has actually reached an internal consensus. Today, I think the Islamic Republic is ruled by a unity government and some of the factionals in that has historically bedeviled the theocracy has at least for now been set aside.

For the first time in the three decades of the existence of the Islamic Republic it is not troubled by divisions and dissension that have plagued previous governments. So I am not quite sure if President Rouhani is under the type of pressure that he speaks about.

However, I think going into these negotiations there are many advantages that the Western powers have, particularly the United States, and one of those advantages are raised expectations. There has been a lot of raised expectations.

Both parties—United States and Iran—have unwisely at times raised expectations about a possible deal and fed a media narrative of a potential historical breakthrough between the two old nemesis.

Suddenly, the hard-pressed Iranian public has come to expect imminent financial relief should the negotiations not yield an agreement. Then Supreme Leader Ali Khamenei, not President Obama, would have a popular backlash at his hand. A disenfranchised dispossessed population is an explosive political problem for the Iranian leadership.

Therefore, I think the Western powers should not be afraid to suspend negotiations or walk away from the table should Iran prove intransigence. Ironically, a stalemate in negotiations are likely to pressure Iran into offering more concessions rather than the United States.

I want to highlight briefly that what we are dealing with here is not necessarily just nuclear infractions but also the Islamic Republic's regional policies. The Islamic Republic remains a revisionist state that has done much to imperil American interests in the Middle East, as was just mentioned.

It has been recently fashionable to suggest that the two parties have an interest in the rise of ISIL and that could essentially offer a pathway for cooperation. On the surface, this may seem sensible.

Both parties do have an interest in defanging the militant Sunni group.

However, the essential axiom of Middle East politics has always been that the enemy of my enemy is still my enemy. The ebbs and flows of war on terrorism should not be allowed to conceal the fact that the Iranian regime and its attempt to upend the regional order remains the United States' most consequential long-term challenge.

The Islamic Republic is not a normal nation state seeking to realize its legitimate aspirations within the existing international system. It is a country whose leadership tends to put premium on conspiracies to explain its predicament, and as was mentioned it has been a staple of Ali Khamenei's speeches that United States is a declining power whose domestic sources of strength are fast eroding.

Finally, the United States and Iran tend to see the region from opposite ends. The Islamic Republic's ideological compulsions and sheer opportunism makes it an unlikely ally for the West.

The coincidence of mutual interest in opposition to a radical Sunni group should not blind us to the enduring threat that the Iranian regime represents to its population and to the region at large.

Thank you.

[The prepared statement of Mr. Takeyh follows:]

COUNCIL on FOREIGN RELATIONS

Iranian Nuclear Talks: Negotiating a Bad Deal?

Prepared Statement by

Ray Takeyh

Senior Fellow for Middle East Studies, Council on Foreign Relations

Hearing before the Subcommittee on Terrorism, Non-Proliferation and Trade
United States House of Representatives
July 16, 2014.

On the surface, the Islamic Republic of Iran has hardly been a responsible actor in the conduct of its foreign relations. A regime that is deeply embedded in Syria's civil war and has embraced terrorism as an instrument of statecraft would seemingly be at a disadvantage in presenting its case to the international community. Yet, Iran has had some success imposing its narrative on the negotiations Iranian officials and the Western nations are conducting about its nuclear program. The theocratic state's "right" to enrich has already been acknowledged in practice if not in principle. The Islamic Republic continues to denounce the numerous U.N. Security Council Resolutions as politically-contrived documents without authority or legitimacy. Thus far, there is little indication that the so-called 5 plus 1 countries are demanding a suspension of Iran's nuclear activities as demanded by the Security Council. And Iran is reported to insist on sustaining its existing enrichment capacity which has placed it well on the road toward nuclear empowerment. The great power's diplomacy will be judged not by clever formulations they devise to accommodate Iran's "red-lines" but by their ability to veer Tehran away from its maximalist positions.

President Hassan Rouhani has managed to inculcate the notion that he is under pressure from the hard-liners at home and that a failure by the West to invest in his presidency would end Iran's moderate interlude. The implication is that time is of the essence, and the West should not miss an opportunity to deal with pragmatists who seek an arms control breakthrough. In essence, the only manner of fortifying the forces of moderation in Iran is for the West to make nuclear concessions.

But a more careful examination reveals that the Islamic Republic has reached an internal consensus. It is ruled today by a unity government. The factionalism that has historically bedeviled the theocracy has, for now, been set aside. For the first-time in its three-decades of existence, the Islamic Republic is not troubled by divisions and dissensions that have undermined previous governments.

For Iran's Supreme Leader, Ayatollah Ali Khamenei, the most important objective is the survival of the regime and preservation of its ideological character. As an astute student of history, Khamenei senses that disunity among the elites can feed popular discontent and imperil the regime. The fraudulent presidential election of 2009 caused not only a legitimacy crisis but also divided the regime's elites. By conceding to Rouhani's election, Khamenei has managed to restore a measure of accountability to the system and has drawn some of his disgruntled cadre back to the fold. Given such domestic calculations, Rouhani's political fortunes are not necessarily contingent on the success of his arms-control policy. Khamenei clearly hopes that his president can ease Iran's economic distress, but the notion that Rouhani will be displaced unless he can quickly obtain concessions from the West is spurious.

Another issue that can paradoxically redound to U.S. advantage is the raised expectations for a deal by November 24th or potentially beyond. To be fair, both Iranian and U.S. officials have unwisely raised expectations and fed a media narrative of a potential historical breakthrough between the two old nemeses. Suddenly, the hard-pressed Iranian public has come to expect imminent financial relief. Should the negotiations not yield an accord in a timely manner, it is Khamenei, not President Obama, who would face a popular backlash. A disenfranchised and dispossessed population is an explosive political problem for Khamenei. The Western powers should not be afraid to suspend negotiations or walk away, should the Iranians prove intransigent. Ironically, stalemated negotiations are likely to pressure Iran into offering more concessions.

More than Just Nuclear Infractions

Although Iran's nuclear ambitions have garnered much attention, the Islamic Republic remains a revisionist state that has done much to imperil core American interests in the Middle East. It has lately been fashionable to suggest that the rise of ISIL offers a pathway for cooperation between the United States and Iran. On the surface, this may seem sensible, as both Washington and Tehran have an interest in defanging a militant Sunni group. But we would be wise to heed the essential axiom of Middle East politics: the enemy of my enemy is still my enemy. The ebbs and flows of the war on terrorism should not be allowed to conceal the fact that the theocratic regime and its attempt to upend the regional order remains the United States most consequential long-term challenge in the Middle East.

The Islamic Republic is not a normal nation-state seeking to realize its legitimate interests but an ideological entity mired in manufactured conspiracies. A persistent theme of Khamenei's speeches is that the United States is a declining power whose domestic sources of strength are fast eroding. In today's disorderly region, Iran sees a unique opportunity to project its influence and undermine the United States and its system of alliances.

In Afghanistan, in the aftermath of the 9/11 attacks, the misapprehension was born that the United States needed Iran's assistance to rehabilitate its war-torn charge, and this misbegotten notion has since migrated from crisis to crisis. The tactical assistance that Iran offered in Afghanistan in 2001 was largely motivated by its fears of being the next target of U.S. retribution. Even Rouhani's own memoirs reflect how concerned and fearful the Islamic Republic was once U.S. forces deposed Saddam's regime in three-weeks. Once Tehran was convinced that America was dragged into a quagmire of its own making, it proceeded to lacerate U.S. forces in both Iraq and Afghanistan by providing munitions and sanctuaries to various militias. In the meantime, Tehran sought steadily to subvert America's allies in the Persian Gulf and to undermine the security of Israel. The Islamic Republic remains the most generous benefactor to both Hamas and Hezbollah who have done much to menace the state of Israel.

Today, in the two central battlefields of the Middle East—Syria and Iraq—Iran's interests are inimical to those of the United States. Iran's stake in Syria has been made clear by its provisions of money, oil, arms, advisors and, most important, Hezbollah shock-troops to prop up the regime of Bashar al-Assad. The United States' interests, meanwhile, strongly argue against working with Iran against ISIL lest we lose the very Sunni support that will be necessary to eradicate that group. By taking a firm stand in Syria against both Assad and ISIL, we can send a strong signal to Iran's leaders that the price of its troublemaking is going to rise.

Similarly in Iraq, any putative alliance with Iran would undo much of what the United States has attempted to accomplish there—the creation of a pluralistic, unitary state that does not represent a threat to itself or its neighbors and which is not a base for terrorism. The only way that President Obama's objective of not only "degrading" but also "destroying" the Islamic State can be achieved is by taking back, over time, much of the territory seized by its fighters in the

Sunni provinces. This will require not only airstrikes in support of the Kurdish troops and Iraqi forces but also significant buy-in from the Sunni tribes who formed the backbone of the uprising against al-Qaeda during the surge. In addition, the sine qua non of the administration's policy is an inclusive government in Iraq that can draw support from neighboring Sunni states such as Saudi Arabia and the United Arab Emirates. Both of these will be unattainable if there is a perception that the United States is seeking a de facto alliance with Iran.

During the past decade, and over two administrations, the United States has been effective in estranging Iran from its European and even Asian customers. But Washington has not affected Iran's position in the Middle East to the same degree. Beyond arms sales to Arab states and attempts to assuage Israeli concerns, the United States has not undertaken a systematic effort to isolate Iran in its immediate neighborhood. Instead of pursuing the chimera of cooperation with the likes of Khamenei, Washington should contest all of Iran's regional assets. From the Shia slums of Baghdad to the battlefields of Syria, Iran should be confronted with a new, inhospitable reality as it searches for partners and collaborators.

The United States and Iran stand at opposite ends of the spectrum in Middle East politics. The Islamic Republic's ideological compulsions and sheer opportunism make it an unlikely ally for the West. The coincidence of mutual opposition to a radical Sunni terrorist group should not blind us to the enduring threat that the mullahs represent.

Iran's Negotiating Style

As the November 24th deadline looms, there is a peculiar concern that Congress can derail the negotiations through bluster and legislation. There are calls for rushing the talks and presenting a skeptical Congress with a deal before they assume their majority. On the surface it seems unusual to worry about the longevity of a diplomatic process that thus far lasted over a decade. Still, no matter what Congress does the Islamic Republic will not walk away from the negotiating table. Given how nuclear diplomacy serves Iran's many interests, Congress is unlikely to disrupt the on-going talks.

Since the exposure of its illicit nuclear program in 2002, Iran's main intention has been to legitimize its expanding atomic infrastructure. The record reveals that Iran's cagy diplomats have gone far in achieving that objective. Although numerous U.N. Security Council resolutions have enjoined Iran to suspend all of its nuclear activities, there is little interest by the great powers to enforce the injunctions that they themselves crafted in the first place. This is an impressive accomplishment for a state that not only defies the U.N. Security Council but also thwarts the International Atomic Energy Agency's attempt to gain access to its scientists and sites. So long as Iran stays at the table it can count on further Western indulgences.

The Islamic Republic has also gained much in non-nuclear sectors from its continued participation in the talks. The clerical regime's dismal human rights record and its harsh repression of its citizens are rarely mentioned by the Western chancelleries. A standard practice of America's Cold War summitry was to press the cause of dissidents in all encounters with Soviet representatives. Given fears that Iran's hyper-sensitive mullahs would abjure nuclear compromises should their domestic abuses be highlighted, the Western diplomats have gone out of their way in assuring their interlocutors that they recognize the clerical regime as a legitimate international actor. The nuclear talks and the prospects of an accord conveniently shield the Supreme Leader Ali Khamenei's repressive state from censure and criticism.

The Islamic Republic today is an aggressive state on the march in the Middle East. Through its proxies and aid it is propping up the Assad regime in Syria and enabling its genocidal war against its citizens. Iran is the most consequential external actor in Iraq and has been instrumental in pressing its Shia allies to reject substantial inclusion of Sunnis in Iraq's governing structure. In the Gulf, Tehran continues to press for eviction of U.S. presence, appreciating that only America's armada stands in the way of its hegemonic ambitions. Terrorism remains an instrument of Iran's statecraft, particularly against Israel. Yet, there is a reluctance to push back on Iran in the increasingly chaotic Middle East for the fear that such a move would undermine the nuclear talks.

In the coming weeks, the diplomats will try hard to craft a nuclear agreement with Iran. They may succeed or they may extend the talks beyond their own self-imposed deadline. In the meantime, they will warn the Iranians that time is running out and various windows are about to slam shot. They will fret about how Congress can foreclose diplomacy by pressing its claims and maybe even passing sanctions measures. The task at hand will be to keep Iranians at the table and the Congress at bay. All this misses the point that the Islamic Republic participates in the talks because they serve so many of its interests. And one of those interests may yet be an accord that eases its path toward nuclear empowerment.

Mr. POE. Perfect timing. The Chair recognizes Mr. McInnis for 5 minutes.

STATEMENT OF MR. J. MATTHEW MCINNIS, RESIDENT FELLOW, AMERICAN ENTERPRISE INSTITUTE

Mr. McINNIS. Thank you, Chairman Poe, Ranking Member Sherman and distinguished members of the House Committee on Foreign Affairs.

Thank you for inviting me here to testify on the current ongoing Iran nuclear negotiations. As has already been noted, prospects for an actual agreement on the 24th of November are dim but I do not underestimate the desire on both sides to get a deal.

We may yet see a breakthrough but I think it is doubtful. While I strongly support finding a diplomatic solution to the impasse with Iran, I also share your concern that this eagerness on our part may cause us to settle for a deal that has not sufficiently addressed the challenge of their program.

I fear since the beginning we have not fully understood what was driving Iran to the table and underestimated our leverage once they got there. It is a recipe for a very frustrating diplomacy.

So what is Iran's calculus here? Most importantly, we should remember there has been no sign—and I think this has been noted here before—no sign of real change in their nuclear policy.

They still want to man a robust Iranian enrichment program that is far beyond what is needed for civilian purposes. They have shown no willingness to come clean on the possible military dimensions of their nuclear research.

If Iran had had a true change of heart we could have resolved all the outstanding concerns a long time ago. Iran would have flung open the doors of Parchin military complex to IAEA inspectors.

That is not the case here. This is not South Africa. This is not Libya. The new diplomatic approach adopted by the supreme leader and President Rouhani is notable but at its heart it is a tactical move.

They may accept some limits on the output of the program but no actual reversal of technological achievements and capabilities will be allowed. This is why we keep stumbling over their red lines, refusing to dismantle any part of their nuclear infrastructure.

However, the supreme leader and President Rouhani and the rest of the Iranian leadership have decided they need to get out from underneath the sanctions and I agree with my colleague, Dr. Takeyh here, on his assessment of the internal dynamics inside the regime right now.

The short and long term economic challenges are just too great for them. They need this deal now and, frankly, they need it more than we do and we don't take advantage of that.

So what are the basics of an acceptable deal? They are quite simple and I think we have discussed them already in the opening statements—a reasonably verifiable regime administered by the IAEA that ensures Iran cannot pursue a nuclear weapon with a clear mechanism to reimpose sanctions for noncompliance.

My colleague, David Albright, will certainly go into much more of the technical discussions about things that we need to address.

But first I want to highlight a couple of things I am concerned about.

First, we need to be aware of the trap of centrifuge numbers. As the efficiency of Iran's centrifuges improve, actual quantities of the machines will matter less. We need to have the right metrics for any type of deal on that topic.

Second, for me, the heart of the matter, really, is bringing Iran into compliance with the IAEA on the possible military dimensions. There should be no relief in the most critical sanctions without resolving this issue satisfactorily.

Third, given the long history of Iran's nuclear activity being exposed rather than willingly acknowledged, the need for a rigorous verification regime goes without saying. There is not trust here, just verify.

Since there was a real risk of additional covert enrichment or weapons development activity, the ban of critical technologies, especially for missiles, needs to be maintained to the greatest degree possible.

Fourth, we need to be very careful about how sanctions are unravelled. Many sanctions are related to Iran's nuclear program even if they are also tied to the regime's support for terrorism and human rights violations.

The reverse is also true. Unthoughtful relaxation of financial sanctions, for example, could prove a great boon to the Islamic Revolutionary Guard Corp's activities across the region.

And that brings me to my final point and, again, agreeing with my colleague, Dr. Takeyh, we should not be looking to use the nuke negotiations as a stepping stone, as a confidence-building measure toward greater cooperation with Iran, unless we see real changes in their behaviors, which I do not expect under this supreme leader.

Tehran is still trying to overhaul the political system in the region through subversive and violent means. It is still supporting and building proxy forces beholden to Iran, designed to threaten the U.S. and our allies and ensure the capacity to execute terrorism missions worldwide.

This includes groups like Lebanese Hezbollah, Palestinian Islamic jihad, Hamas and, most recently, the Houthis on the march in Yemen. Our end states for Syria and Iraq are different. We may have some form of deconfliction with Quds Force Commander Qasem Soleimani against ISIS on the ground in Iraq. We may even have some form of detente. But this is not rapprochement. Until we see actual shifts in the policy from the supreme leader, our negotiations, our sanctions strategies and our regional policies need to be very sober.

We should recognize at best we are checking the regime's worst behavior while we wait for real change in Tehran.

Thank you.

[The prepared statement of Mr. McInnis follows:]

J. Matthew McInnis
American Enterprise Institute

Testimony before the House Foreign Affairs Committee
Joint Subcommittee on Terrorism, Nonproliferation, and Trade
November 18, 2014

AVOIDING A BAD NUCLEAR DEAL WITH IRAN

Parameters of an acceptable deal

Recent indications from the P5+1 (the U.S., United Kingdom, France, Germany, Russia and China) negotiations with Iran over their nuclear program imply a complete comprehensive agreement is unlikely by the self-imposed deadline of November 24. Very significant obstacles appear to remain on limiting Iranian uranium enrichment capacity, sequencing of any sanctions removal, the duration of a new monitoring regime and compliance with outstanding concerns of the International Atomic Energy Association about the possible military dimensions of Iran's program. Most likely we will see another extension of the talks, possibly with a revised framework for an eventual agreement based on the Joint Plan of Action (JPA) signed in Geneva in November 2013.

However, both sides have also signaled that they are very keen to reach a deal, so we may yet witness a successful last-minute effort to reach a solution. Under these circumstances, such an achievement would justifiably raise questions whether reaching an agreement in itself is taking precedence over the P5+1's objective to prevent an Iranian nuclear weapon. This would be a recipe for a bad deal.

So what would be a good agreement, one that is truly in the U.S.' and our allies' interests? At the core, the parameters of an acceptable deal are quite simple: a reasonably verifiable regime administered by the IAEA that ensures Iran cannot pursue a nuclear weapon, with a clear mechanism to re-impose sanctions for non-compliance. Breaking it down further, here are the main components of a final agreement the U.S. should be insisting on.

- Extending the amount of time Iran would need to produce weapons-grade uranium with existing stockpiles sufficient for one nuclear bomb (i.e. breakout) to 6-12 months. With Iran's existing technology, this has arguably meant reducing (dismantling, not unplugging) the number of Iran's existing centrifuges to at least below 5,000, and ideally below 2,000, from their current approximately 19,000 installed. But given Iran's centrifuge efficiency will improve as its infrastructure modernizes, we likely need to think in different metrics to ensure sufficient warning time for a breakout.
- Existing stockpiles of enriched uranium, especially those at 20 percent enrichment as well as natural uranium, need to be further reduced and capped.
- Ensuring Iran has addressed all of the IAEA's concerns about the possible military dimensions of its nuclear program before lifting all of the nuclear-related sanctions.
- Guaranteeing Iran's plutonium pathway to a nuclear bomb is not feasible.

- Maintaining and enforcing measures to block Iran's illicit acquisition of nuclear and missile delivery technologies.
- Ensuring monitoring and compliance regimes for a final agreement are robust and have a long duration, ideally for 15-20 years.
- Preventing nuclear-related sanctions relief from undermining terrorism and human rights related sanctions on Iran.
- Confirming to the greatest degree possible that these restrictions on the Iranian nuclear program are not easily reversible.

Thinking through Iran's Calculus

All of these objectives should be easily achievable and preserve a civilian nuclear program more than adequate for Iran's energy, medical and research needs *if* Tehran is sincere that it has no intention to pursue a nuclear weapon. However, the Islamic Republic has continued to blatantly resist the IAEA's efforts to bring the regime into full compliance with United Nations resolutions and address substantial questions about the program's likely weapons research related activities.

The U.S.' greatest concern during the negotiations should be that Tehran has not actually changed its core nuclear program policies. Certainly since the election of President Hassan Rouhani last year, the regime has demonstrated its desire to find a way out from under the economically crippling sanctions and de-escalate the confrontation with the West over the nuclear issue. Iran has made the strategic decision to seriously talk to the U.S. The regime has not made the strategic decision to normalize its nuclear effort to reflect what a purely civilian program would look like. Otherwise, for example, rather than stonewalling the IAEA, Tehran would be welcoming the agency's inspectors to visit the Parchin Military Complex outside Tehran and other sites widely suspected of nuclear weapons related research.

This is also why there are few, if any, useful analogies in these negotiations to earlier diplomatic resolutions with countries like Libya and South Africa about their nuclear programs. In these two insistences, the respective regimes had made clear breaks in their national policies. This is not the case with Iran. The Supreme Leader and the rest of the leadership have made it very clear that the regime will not fundamentally reverse the achievements of Iran's program, that they will be a nuclear state and that they will continue to advance their technological capabilities.

It is also useful to consider why Iran decided to come to the table in the first place as we evaluate potential next steps in the process and anticipate Tehran's next moves, whether there is a good deal, a bad one or none at all. Though President Rouhani's 2013 campaign platform was largely based on seeking a less confrontational relationship with the West and getting relief from economic sanctions, it surprised many observers that the Supreme Leader largely agreed with Rouhani on need for direct talks with the U.S. Why was Khamenei ready to seriously engage the West?

There are many reasons for Khamenei's support for talks: first, the stronger economic pressures resulting from the harsh sanctions imposed a year earlier (the European oil embargo for example). Second, Khamenei and Rouhani had a long association over the management of Iran's nuclear program. The Supreme Leader had learned to trust the new president and had faith in him as a negotiator. Third,

Iran had realized long before the breakout of ISIS that rising Sunni extremism and the deepening sectarian conflict emanating from Syria were becoming an even greater threat to its regime than the need for a potential nuclear deterrent against the United States and Israel (nuclear weapons are unlikely to be useful in fighting extremist groups like ISIS and al Qaeda for example) and would require greater focus and resources. Fourth, the Iranian leadership perceived President Obama's strong desire to break the impasse on the nuclear program, including moving away from demands for zero uranium enrichment. Fifth, the relative strategic value of a possible nuclear weapon was declining for Iran as its conventional deterrence capabilities improved, especially as Iran's maritime defenses and ballistic missiles were enhanced and upgraded. Finally, and perhaps most importantly for the nuclear negotiations, Iran's nuclear program had finally reached a level of technical competency that could no longer be reversed.

As a result of these factors, Iran found itself with negotiating room. As long as the Islamic Republic is able to produce easily and rapidly more highly enriched uranium, it can give up some of its supply with relative ease.

This is also why the negotiations continue to hit major obstacles. Real reversals in the nuclear program's capability to produce enriched uranium would undermine one of the main motives of the Iranian regime to engage in talks. But reducing Iran's capability to produce enriched uranium is exactly what the U.S. and other P5+1 countries have been seeking as the best way to ensure Iran cannot breakout undetected.

When the talks under the JPA hit their initial July 20 deadline, the decision to extend negotiations into November was easy for Iran. All the incentives remained in place for Iran to work toward a deal and the Supreme Leader has continued to express his support for Rouhani's efforts. Above all, Tehran didn't want to go backwards in the process and face the return of full sanctions.

In fact, we are arguably seeing increasing anxiousness on the part of the Iranians to get a deal since July, even if real concessions have not materialized from Tehran. Perhaps the recent substantial drop in oil prices may have convinced Rouhani and the senior leadership that their critical domestic economic reform programs are in potential serious jeopardy and that sanctions relief must happen soon. That is not to mention the conflict with ISIS, which is bleeding valuable Iranian resources. Even fears of the Israelis starting a covert campaign against Iran's nuclear facilities may have spooked the regime's leadership.

As we approach the next deadline on November 24 these factors and incentives are the reason why, from Tehran's perspective, another interim agreement or extension is the most likely near term outcome.

Dangers of a bad deal

What if we get a bad deal, one that removes the most important sanctions but does not extend Iran's breakout scenario to at least six months, that does not address the possible military dimensions of Iran's nuclear work, that does not allow for rigorous monitoring and transparency, that places only short duration constraints that are easily reversible, and that unravels sanctions against Iran's support for terrorism and gross human rights violations as well?

Most critically, a bad deal leaves everyone in the region uncertain about Iran's intentions and potential nuclear weapons capabilities. Our commitment to effectively detect, respond and deter Tehran should they secretly pursue a nuclear weapon will also be more suspect to our partners. Uncertainty and insecurity will breed potentially dangerous decisions by our allies, including the pursuit of nuclear weapons by Saudi Arabia and Turkey or new security relationships that could oppose our interests, such as the Gulf States making strategic accommodation with Iran.

A bad deal will also leave Iran flush with cash to pursue its objectives in Iraq, the Levant, Yemen, Afghanistan, Africa and elsewhere, objectives which in the long-term almost always oppose ours. We will have much reduced leverage to push back.

In the worst case scenario, we could to eventually face a nuclear Iran, for whom classic containment and deterrence approaches are unlikely to be effective.

Policy implications

Aside from ensuring the United States actually gets a good deal, how can the U.S. administration and Congress avoid a bad deal? We should:

- Recognize Iran needs this deal more than we do and act like it. Western negotiators should be playing tough, understanding that they, rather than the Iranians, have had the stronger position all along.
- Communicate clearly that any deal containing significant suspension or removal of sanctions should have 'snap back' penalties if Iran violates the agreement. The U.S. should reinforce Iran's fears of returning to the status quo ante, prior to the JPA, with full sanctions and even the military option on the table.
- Congress and the Administration should have a thorough, even public discussion on what sanctions will remain on Iran if a nuclear deal is fully implemented. In particular, too liberal relief of the nuclear-related financial sanctions could provide an unwanted boon to the Islamic Revolutionary Guard Corps and Quds Force. Congress and the Administration should also reinforce that any relaxing of sanctions against Iran for its support for terrorism and gross human rights violations are dependent on separate measurable changes in those behaviors and will not be connected to a potential nuclear deal.
- We must diligently reassure our allies that we are committed to preventing Iran from getting a nuclear weapon lest we trigger a dangerous realignment of security relationships in the region and a potential nuclear arms race.
- Work to ensure our diplomatic missions, foreign partners and intelligence community will be able to provide a robust monitoring capability if a new agreement is implemented. Verification is the only way this works.

Finally U.S. policymakers and negotiators need to have a very sober understanding that Iran is only demonstrating it wants to de-escalate its confrontation with the West by coming to the table over the nuclear issue and engage tactically with the U.S. on issues like the Islamic State because it benefits Tehran's own near-term interests. Iran has shown no signs of an actual strategic shift in its core ideology to oppose U.S. interests in the region. President Rouhani is still a creature of the Islamic Republic and, so far at least, pursues policies intended to preserve the regime rather than fundamentally change it. The Revolution is not over.

———————

Mr. POE. The Chair recognizes Mr. Albright for 5 minutes his opening statement.

STATEMENT OF MR. DAVID ALBRIGHT, PRESIDENT, INSTITUTE FOR SCIENCE AND INTERNATIONAL SECURITY

Mr. ALBRIGHT. Thank you, Chairman Poe and Ranking Member Sherman, for the opportunity to testify today.

I would like to just go through several points, really, headlines of what I see is important to consider today in this deal.

First, I think a long-term deal, if carefully crafted, can keep Iran from building nuclear weapons. But getting that deal is a major challenge, particularly by November 24th. If not achieved, the interim deal will need to be extended, and that brings me to my second point.

The interim deal has accomplished many worthwhile goals, as Mr. Sherman has pointed out, but it appears to be fraying at the edges and needs to be strengthened if it is to continue being effective. We work on the technical side of this and we noticed in the last International Atomic Energy Agency report that some of the expectations of the interim deal have not been met. One is that Iran started to enrich for the first time in an advanced centrifuge called the IR–5.

I know we relayed those concerns to the administration pretty early on Friday and the administration got a commitment by Iran that weekend that it would stop. Whether it will continue to stop, we don't know. Iran continues to or still needs to oxidize at least 500 kilograms of newly produced 3.5 percent LEU that they produced, and this was produced since the July extension.

Also, Iran had said it would convert 25 kilograms of the near 20 percent LU oxide into fuel assemblies. From the IAEA data, only 5 kilograms have actually been turned into fuel assemblies and I think we don't view these as violations of the deal since they still have until November 24th. But to us and ISIS it represents a fraying of the deal and so—even if it is extended—these things need to be addressed.

The third issue I want to discuss, and I won't spend much time on it because I think we are all in agreement, is that, there has been little progress on getting Iran to address the IAEA conditions and I will just say that there needs to be at least concrete progress on that issue before a deal is signed.

Obviously, Iran can't address all the IAEA's issues prior to November 24th and, in fact, the IAEA director general has said Iran isn't even trying.

But the negotiators should only sign a deal if Iran has made some concrete progress and that can be anything from allowing visits to the military sites such as Parchin to some kind of international recognition that Iran had a nuclear weapons program and then others can think of other things.

Later on, Iran is going to have to address the IAEA issues and some sanctions are going to have to be tied to that. I don't know what the U.S. is thinking on that but I would hope that there are very significant sanctions tied to actually addressing those issues.

Another issue that we have worked on extensively in the last several months has been the sanctions on what we call proliferation sensitive goods. They have got to stay in place during the length of the agreement or through at least most of it until Iran has demonstrated that it is in full compliance and things are going well. And in particular, U.N. Security Council sanctions on such goods need to remain in place.

Iran is not expected to stop seeking proliferation-sensitive goods abroad for its missile and other military programs. It may seek goods abroad for its clandestine nuclear activities and facilities.

It is certainly doing so today. Iran's regime is well known to European authorities, including the Germans, for constantly trying to break their laws. In 2012 and 2013, more than two-thirds of their 264 investigations in Germany were involving the Islamic Republic. And Germany expects the proportion to remain the same this year. So Iran is a habitual sanctions violator and that is not expected to change.

Now, if the sanctions legislation or sanctions continue through the U.N. Security Council resolutions there will be a need to provide goods to authorized nuclear programs, whatever level of those programs that remain, and the precedent for that is the exemption created for the Bushehr reactor and that exemption can be applied to an authorized nuclear programs.

The difference between the Bushehr exception and any newly authorized exports would be that that channel or procurement channel is going to have to be monitored extremely carefully and involve the U.N. panel of experts, the International Atomic Energy Agency and supplier states.

The fifth point I want to address is that I think we have all agreed that Iran should have a limited number of centrifuges. My group probably has one of the high numbers. We would accept up to 4,000 IR–1s and view that level can be verified.

Now, the important way to strengthen that goal is also to reduce the stocks of low-enriched uranium and there has been discussion in the media about how the administration plans to remove large amounts of the stocks from Iran. I think that is a workable proposition but it should not substitute for the reduction in numbers of centrifuges—it should strengthen that goal but it should not substitute for the goal of achieving low numbers of centrifuges.

And I just want to close by mentioning that Congressman Sherman mentioned uranium ore. That often does not receive the attention it needs.

The administration has told me in the past that they are seeking limitations on uranium ore but we will see if that happens. But it requires not only knowing how much they made it total, but also knowing how much they are making every year, how much they have stockpiled, their past illicit efforts to acquire uranium internationally and then to cap that uranium in a way that Iran would not have more uranium on hand inside the country than it needs——

Mr. POE. Conclude your remarks, please.

Mr. ALBRIGHT [continuing]. It needs to meet its actual needs.

Thank you. Sorry.

Mr. POE. Thank you.

Mr. ALBRIGHT. Sorry for going over.

[The prepared statement of Mr. Albright follows:]

"Iranian Nuclear Talks"

Testimony of David Albright, President
Institute for Science and International Security (ISIS)
before the
Terrorism, Nonproliferation, and Trade Subcommittee,
Committee on Foreign Affairs,
U.S. House of Representatives

November 18, 2014

Iran and the P5+1 group of countries (the United States, Britain, France, Germany, Russia, and China) are feverishly working to reach a final, comprehensive solution on Iran's nuclear program before the November 24, 2014 extended deadline of the Joint Plan of Action (JPA). The November 2013 JPA set out a process aimed at limiting Iran's nuclear program in exchange for relief from economic and financial sanctions. On a separate but linked negotiating track, Iran and the International Atomic Energy Agency (IAEA) have been working on a step-wise approach to address the IAEA's concerns, particularly those about the alleged past and possibly on-going military dimensions (or so-called PMD) of Iran's nuclear program. However, this process has stalled. Whether and how Iran complies with the IAEA's concerns is currently being played out in the context of P5+1/Iran negotiations.

Despite hopeful signs of progress in the negotiations, much reportedly remains to be settled. If there is no deal, an extension of the JPA may occur while the parties attempt to continue to reach agreement. And if negotiations fail, the United States will likely face a daunting challenge of preventing the escalation of tensions while attempting to pressure Iran back to the negotiating table. The potential for the parties to commit to a bad deal that actually worsens tensions and mistrust in the long run is likewise a dangerous prospect. In order to avoid a bad deal, the P5+1 must hold strong on achieving an agreement that limits Iran's nuclear program to a reasonable civilian capability, significantly increases the timelines for breakout to nuclear weapons, and introduces enhanced verification that goes beyond the IAEA's Additional Protocol. A sound deal will also require Iran to verifiably address the IAEA's concerns about its past and possibly on-going work on nuclear weapons, which means Iran must address those concerns in a concrete manner before a deal is finalized or any relief of economic or financial sanctions occurs.

Primary Goal of a Deal

The primary goal of a comprehensive solution is to ensure that Iran's nuclear program is indeed peaceful, against a background of two decades of Iran deceiving the IAEA about its nuclear programs, including military nuclear programs. This long history of deception and violations places additional burdens on achieving a verifiable, long term agreement. To achieve a verifiable solution, Iran will need to limit specific, existing nuclear capabilities, including reducing significantly the number of its centrifuges and the size of its uranium and low enriched uranium stocks, and limiting its centrifuge R&D programs. As mentioned above, Iran should demonstrate in a concrete manner its intention to address allegations of past and possibly on-going work on nuclear weapons prior to the finalization of any deal. The agreement will need to include verification provisions that create a critical baseline of information, including how many centrifuges Iran has made, how much natural uranium it has produced and is producing annually, and its inventory of raw materials and equipment for its centrifuge program. This baseline is necessary if the agreement is to provide assurances about the absence of secret nuclear activities and facilities. Sanctions on proliferation sensitive goods will need to continue and will need to be enforced rigorously, while allowing exemptions for authorized nuclear programs. Iran will need to allow mechanisms to ensure that any further military nuclear related work would be detected on short order. Without these limitations on Iran's nuclear programs and expanded verification conditions, a long-term deal will likely fail or exacerbate the threat from Iran. However, an adequate agreement is possible and within reach of the United States and its negotiating partners.

Adequate Reaction Time

A key goal of the negotiations is to ensure that any deal provides adequate reaction time, namely, adequate time to respond diplomatically and internationally to stop Iran if it does decide to renege on its commitments and build nuclear weapons. According to Undersecretary of State Wendy Sherman, "We must be confident that any effort by Tehran to break out of its obligations will be so visible and time-consuming that the attempt would have no chance of success."[1] That goal must be at the core of any agreement.

Obtaining adequate reaction time requires that limitations are placed on Iran's sensitive nuclear programs, adequate verification is ensured, and concrete progress has been demonstrated that Iran will address the IAEA's concerns about its past and possibly on-going nuclear weapons efforts. Because of Iran's long history of non-compliance with its safeguards obligations, a deal must last long enough, on order of 20 years, so that there is little risk of Iran seeking nuclear weapons.

Covering all Breakout Paths to the Bomb.

If Iran were to make the political decision to produce a nuclear weapon after a comprehensive nuclear deal, it is not possible to second guess how it may proceed. Iran may use its declared nuclear facilities to secretly make enough highly enriched uranium (HEU) or plutonium for a bomb or it may build covert sites to make the HEU or separate the plutonium. Given that Iran has such a long history of building and conducting secret nuclear activities, U.S. negotiators need to take a broad view and secure a deal that makes all of Iran's paths to the bomb a time consuming, risky effort.

Some have advocated that only the covert route to nuclear weapons is likely. Those who favor this view often rely on the U.S. 2007 National Intelligence Estimate, *Iran: Nuclear Intentions and Capabilities*. It concluded, "We assess with moderate confidence that Iran probably would

---

[1] "Iran's Current Enrichment Level Not Acceptable: US," Agence France Presse. September 17, 2014.

use covert facilities—rather than its declared nuclear sites—for the production of highly enriched uranium for a weapon." That assessment may have been true in 2007 when Iran had few centrifuges, and in fact, we now know, was building a covert centrifuge plant at Qom, called the Fordow facility. However, that statement no longer holds true.

At this point in time, it is unlikely that Iran would rely entirely on the covert pathway option for fear of getting caught again as it did in building the formerly secret Fordow facility, and long before it has enough weapon-grade uranium or separated plutonium for nuclear weapons. The revelation about the Qom enrichment plant was highly damaging to Iran's international credibility. For example, Russia became much more critical of Iran after this revelation and the creation of damaging sanctions became easier. Therefore, Iran is unlikely to want to repeat that mistake without greater assurance of being able to successfully hide a covert program, something it likely lacks now and will not gain anytime soon if the long term deal is carefully crafted by the United States and its partners.

Iran is more likely today to choose a safe route to preserving and further developing a capability to produce fissile material for a nuclear weapon. In the case of gas centrifuges, it is likely to seek to maintain and increase its capabilities at declared centrifuge sites, the associated centrifuge manufacturing complex, and centrifuge R&D facilities. It would view this path as the preferred one, because it can simply and legitimately claim that all its activities are civil in nature, even if it is actually hiding the goal of eventually seeking nuclear weapons. If it opts to make nuclear weapons in the future, its declared programs could serve as the basis of whatever it does. Then, it could pursue breakout as it deems most appropriate, whether by misusing its declared centrifuge facilities, building covert ones, or using both paths together.

Thus, the U.S. goal should be limiting sharply the number of centrifuges at declared sites and constraining centrifuge manufacturing and R&D activities, both of which could help outfit covert programs. This approach would greatly diminish Iran's ability to breakout to nuclear weapons. If Iran decides to build nuclear weapons in the future, it would have to start from this relatively low level of capability, regardless of the path it would actually select in the future. The long timeline to acquire enough HEU for a weapon may turn out to deter Iran from even trying.

This strategy depends on creating a robust verification regime able to detect covert nuclear activities or a small hidden away centrifuge plant. Iran has assuredly learned from its mistakes at hiding the Qom enrichment site. In fact, it has likely developed more sophisticated methods to hide covert nuclear activities. But robust verification, which requires measures beyond the Additional Protocol, can provide assurance that Iran is not hiding centrifuge plants or other nuclear capabilities in the future. These additional verification measures would ensure that Iran would have a very hard time creating or maintaining a covert program outside of its declared programs after signing a long term agreement.

It is wiser to anticipate and block all of Iran's potential future paths to the bomb, rather than guessing and choosing the wrong one.

Quantifying Adequate Response Time: The Role of Breakout Calculations

One assured way to quantify the concept of adequate reaction time when discussing limitations on uranium enrichment programs is to link timely reaction time to breakout time. Breakout time is the amount of time Iran would need to create enough weapon-grade uranium for a single nuclear weapon, if it reneged or cheated on the agreement. Additional time would be needed to fabricate the nuclear weapon itself but the creation of enough fissile material (weapon-grade uranium or separated plutonium) is widely accepted as the "long pole in the tent" of making a nuclear weapon and the only part of this process susceptible to reliable discovery and subsequent pressure. Other nuclear weaponization activities, such as producing high explosive components, electronic components, or uranium metal parts, are notoriously difficult to detect and stop. By focusing on breakout time—as defined above—the agreement would grant the international community a guaranteed period of time to react and prevent Iran's success. The longer the breakout time, the more reaction options we have. A deal that enshrines a short breakout time is risky because if Iran were to make the decision to make a weapon, military intervention would be the only available response.

Thus, time for Iran's ability to produce enough weapon-grade uranium for a bomb must be sufficiently long to allow the international community to prepare and implement a response able to stop Iran from succeeding. Typically, the U.S. negotiators have sought limitations in Iran's nuclear programs that lead to reaction times of twelve months. ISIS has taken the position that under certain conditions six months could be adequate. To better understand the implications of breakout, we have prepared a range of breakout calculations under a wide variety of current and posited centrifuge capabilities that in essence convert the reaction time, i.e. breakout time, into an equivalent number of centrifuges and stocks of low enriched uranium.

One of the calculations considers an important case, namely the current, frozen centrifuge program under the JPA where Iran retains its existing, installed IR-1 centrifuges and no stocks of near 20 percent LEU hexafluoride. In this case, the breakout time is about two months, which is the same as public U.S. government estimates. If the number of IR-1 centrifuges were reduced to about 10,000, breakout time would grow to about three months, according to the ISIS estimates.

To achieve a breakout time of 6-12 months, which is more desirable, the calculations lead to a centrifuge program of about 2,000-4,000 IR-1 centrifuges. Thus, any nuclear deal should allow no more than about 4,000 IR-1 centrifuges.

Sound Negotiating Principles

Beyond technical limitations, the negotiations have shown that the principles driving the positions of the P5+1 differ markedly from those of Iran. Any deal should satisfy the following principles if it is to last:

- Sufficient response time in case of violations;
- A nuclear program meeting Iran's practical needs;
- Adequate irreversibility of constraints;
- Stable provisions; and
- Adequate verification.

These principles flow from the effort to ensure that Iran's nuclear program is peaceful and remains so. These principles also reflect long experience in negotiating arms control and non-proliferation agreements and a recognition of the strengths and weaknesses in those agreements to date.

Iran on the other hand has emphasized the principles of cooperation and transparency. These principles are predicated on its assertion that its word should be trusted, namely its pronouncement that it will not build nuclear weapons. These principles also reflect its long standing view that any agreement should have constrained verification conditions and minimal impact on its nuclear programs, even allowing for their significant growth, despite the current lack of economic or practical justifications for such growth. Many of Iran's negotiating positions have been rejected because they can be undone on short order, offering little practical utility in constraining Iran's future abilities to build nuclear weapons. Iran on numerous occasions in the past has shown a willingness to stop cooperation with the IAEA and reverse agreed upon constraints, sometimes rapidly. A robust and painstakingly built international sanctions regime on Iran cannot be lifted in return for inadequate and reversible constraints.

The negotiating process has shown the complexity of any agreement able to ensure that Iran's nuclear program will remain peaceful. But by sticking to sound principles, potential compromises can be better evaluated and any resulting deal will be more likely to last.

Specific Provisions

In the rest of my testimony, I would like to focus on several specific provisions or goals necessary to a successful deal. In particular, I will discuss the following:

1. **Achieve Concrete Progress in Resolving Concerns about Iran's Past and Possibly Ongoing Nuclear Weapons Efforts**
2. **Maintain Domestic and International Sanctions on Proliferation Sensitive Goods**
3. **Render Excess Centrifuges Less Risky**
4. **Institutionalize a Minimal Centrifuge R&D Program**
5. **Keep Centrifuge Numbers Below about 2,000-4,000 IR-1 Centrifuges and as a Supplementary Measure Achieve Lower Stocks of LEU hexafluoride and oxide**
6. **Beware the concept of "SWU" as a Limit**
7. **Ensure Arak Reactor's Changes are Irreversible**

1) Achieve Concrete Progress in Resolving Concerns about Iran's Past and Possibly Ongoing Nuclear Weapons Efforts

Despite a great effort over the last year, the IAEA has learned little from Iran that has added to the inspectors' ability to resolve their concern about Iran's past nuclear weapons efforts and possibly on-going work related to nuclear weapons. Recently, the IAEA has also been unable to reach agreement with Iran on how to tackle the remaining military nuclear issues. The IAEA has repeatedly emphasized that the military nuclear issues need to be addressed and solved.

For years, the inspectors have unsuccessfully asked the Islamic Republic to address the substantial body of evidence that Iran was developing nuclear weapons prior to 2004 and that it may have continued some of that, or related, work afterwards, even up to the present. Before a deal is concluded, concrete progress is needed on the central issue of whether Iran has worked on nuclear weapons and is maintaining a capability to revive such efforts in the future.

Addressing all of the IAEA's outstanding concerns about Iran's past and possibly on-going military nuclear efforts prior to the November deadline appears unlikely. Nonetheless, without concrete progress, which could take several forms, a deal should not be signed.

Supreme Leader Ali Khamenei often declares that nuclear weapons violate Islamic strictures. His denials are not credible. The United States, its main European allies, and most importantly the IAEA itself, assess that Iran had a sizable nuclear weapons program into 2003. The U.S. intelligence community in the 2007 National Intelligence Estimate (NIE) agreed: "We assess with high confidence that until fall 2003, Iranian military entities were working under government direction to develop nuclear weapons." The Europeans and the IAEA have made clear, the United States less so, that Iran's nuclear weapons development may have continued after 2003, albeit in a less structured manner. In its November 2011 safeguards report, the IAEA provided evidence of Iran's pre- and post-2003 nuclear weaponization efforts. The IAEA found, "There are also indications that some activities relevant to the development of a nuclear explosive device continued after 2003, and that some may still be ongoing." To reinforce this point to Iran, the United States in late August sanctioned Iran's Organization of Defensive Innovation and Research (SPND), which it said is a Tehran-based entity established in early 2011 that is primarily responsible for research in the field of nuclear weapons development. Thus, there is widespread evidence and agreement that Iran has worked on developing nuclear weapons and that some of those activities may have continued to today.

Addressing the IAEA's concerns about the military dimensions of Iran's nuclear programs is fundamental to any long-term agreement. Although much of the debate about an agreement with Iran rightly focuses on Tehran's uranium enrichment and plutonium production capabilities, an agreement that side steps the military issues would risk being unverifiable. Moreover, the world would not be so concerned if Iran had never conducted weaponization activities aimed at building a nuclear weapon. After all, Japan has enrichment activities but this program is not regarded with suspicion. Trust in Iran's intentions, resting on solid verification procedures, is critical to a serious agreement.

A prerequisite for any comprehensive agreement is for the IAEA to know when Iran sought nuclear weapons, how far it got, what types it sought to develop, and how and where it did this work. Was this weapons capability just put on the shelf, waiting to be quickly restarted? The IAEA needs a good baseline of Iran's military nuclear activities, including the manufacturing of equipment for the program and any weaponization related studies, equipment, and locations. The IAEA needs this information to design a verification regime. Moreover, to develop confidence in the absence of these activities—a central mission—the IAEA will need to periodically inspect these sites and interview key individuals for years to come. Without information about past military nuclear work, it cannot know where to go and who to speak to.

The situation today, unless rectified, does not allow for the creation of an adequate verification regime. Moreover, the current situation risks the creation of dangerous precedents for any verification regime that would make it impossible for the IAEA to determine with confidence that nuclear weapons activities are not on-going. Adding verification conditions to any deal is unlikely to help if the fundamental problem is the lack of Iranian cooperation. The IAEA already has the legal right to pursue these questions under the comprehensive safeguards agreement with Iran.

Despite the IAEA's rights under the comprehensive safeguards agreement, Iran has regularly denied the IAEA access to military sites, such as a site at the Parchin complex, a site where high-explosive experiments linked to nuclear triggers may have occurred. Iran has reconstructed much of this site at Parchin, making IAEA verification efforts all but impossible. Tehran has undertaken at this site what looks to most observers as a blatant effort to defeat IAEA verification. However, Parchin is but one of many sites the IAEA wants to inspect as part of its efforts to understand the military dimensions of Iran's nuclear programs. A full Iranian declaration may reveal even more sites of concern.

Iran continues to say no to IAEA requests to interview key individuals, such as Mohsen Fakrizadeh, the suspected military head of the nuclear-weapons program in the early 2000s and perhaps today, and Sayyed Abbas Shahmoradi-Zavareh, former head of the Physics Research Center, alleged to be the central location in the 1990s of Iran's militarized nuclear research. The IAEA interviewed Shahmoradi years ago about a limited number of his suspicious procurement activities conducted through Sharif University of Technology. The IAEA was not fully satisfied with his answers and its dissatisfaction increased once he refused to discuss his activities for the Physics Research Center. Since the initial interviews, the IAEA has obtained far more information about Shahmoradi and the Physics Research Center's procurement efforts. The need to interview both individuals, as well as others, remains.

If Iran is able to successfully evade addressing the IAEA's concerns now, when biting sanctions are in place, why would it address them later when these sanctions are lifted, regardless of anything it may pledge today? Iran's lack of clarity on alleged nuclear weaponization and its noncooperation with the IAEA, if accepted as part of a nuclear agreement, would create a large vulnerability in any future verification regime. How large? Iran would have clear precedents to deny inspectors access to key facilities and individuals. There would be essentially no-go zones across the country for inspectors. Tehran could declare a suspect site a military base and thus off limits. And what better place to conduct clandestine, prohibited activities, such as uranium enrichment and weaponization?

Iran would have also defeated a central tenet of IAEA inspections—the need to determine both the correctness and completeness of a state's nuclear declaration. The history of Iran's previous military nuclear efforts may never come to light and the international community would lack confidence that these capabilities would not emerge in the future. Moreover, Iran's ratification of the Additional Protocol or acceptance of additional verification conditions, while making the IAEA's verification task easier in several important ways, would not solve the basic problem posed by Iran's lack of cooperation on key, legitimate IAEA concerns. Other countries contemplating the clandestine development of nuclear weapons will certainly watch Tehran closely.

Clearly, there is little time for Iran to address all the IAEA's outstanding concerns prior to the November 24 deadline. However, an approach can be implemented whereby Iran can choose to admit to having had a nuclear weapons program, or at least accept a credible, international judgment that it had one, and allow IAEA access to key military sites, such as Parchin, and critical engineers and scientists linked to those efforts. If no such concrete demonstration is forthcoming by the end of November, negotiations should continue, although a deal should not be signed, unless it offers no significant relief from financial and economic sanctions.

2) Maintain Sanctions on Proliferation Sensitive Goods

A comprehensive nuclear agreement is not expected to end Iran's illicit efforts to obtain goods for its missile and other military programs. Iran appears committed to continuing its illicit operations to obtain goods for a range of sanctioned programs. On August 30, 2014, Iranian President Hassan Rouhani stated on Iranian television: "Of course we bypass sanctions. We are proud that we bypass sanctions." Given Iran's sanctions-busting history, a comprehensive nuclear agreement should not include any provisions that would interfere in efforts of the international community to effectively sanction Iranian military programs.

The deal must also create a basis to end, or at least detect with high probability, Iran's illicit procurement of goods for its nuclear programs. Evidence suggests that in the last few years Iran has been conducting its illegal operations to import goods for its nuclear program with greater secrecy and sophistication, regardless of the scale of procurements in the last year or two. A long term nuclear agreement should ban Iranian illicit trade in items for its nuclear programs while creating additional mechanisms to verify this ban. Such a verified ban is a critical part of ensuring that Iran is not establishing the wherewithal to

- Build secret nuclear sites,
- Make secret advances in its advanced centrifuge[2] or other nuclear programs, or
- Surge in capability if it left the agreement.

These conditions argue for continuing all the UNSC and national sanctions and well-enforced export controls on proliferation-sensitive goods. Such goods are those key goods used or needed in Iran's nuclear programs and nuclear weapon delivery systems, the latter typically interpreted as covering ballistic missiles.

Sanctions should continue on the listed goods in the UNSC resolutions, many of them dual-use in nature, and more generally on those other dual-use goods that could contribute to uranium

---

[2] Aside from the IR-2m and a few other centrifuge models, little is known about Iran's next generation centrifuges. Quarterly IAEA safeguards reports indicate that Iran has not successfully operated next generation centrifuges on a continuous basis or in significant numbers since their installation began at the Natanz Pilot Fuel Enrichment Plant. This suggests that Iran may be having difficulty with aspects of their design or operation. Iran's failure to deploy next-generation centrifuges in significant quantities is one indication that sanctions were effective to slow or significantly raise the costs of procurement.

enrichment, plutonium reprocessing, heavy water, and nuclear weapon delivery systems (see United Nations Security Council resolution 1929, par. 13). The latter is often referred to as the "catch-all" provision and mirrors many national catch-all requirements in export control laws and regulations. In the case of Iran, this provision is especially important. Without illicitly obtaining the goods covered by catch-all, Iran would be severely constrained in building or expanding nuclear sites.

The P5+1 powers need to manage carefully the transition to a time when imports of goods to Iran are allowed for legitimate nuclear and later possibly for civilian uses. Many proliferation sensitive goods are dual-use goods, which have applications both in nuclear and non-nuclear industries and institutions. Currently, the world is on heightened alert about Iran's illicit procurements for its sanctioned nuclear, missile, and military programs. Routinely, this alert has led to the thwarting of many illicit purchases and interdictions of banned goods. But as nations enter into expanded commercial and trade relationships with Iran, a risk is that many countries will effectively stand down from this heightened state of awareness and lose much of their motivation to stop banned sales to Iran even if UN sanctions remain in place. Despite the sanctions and vigilant efforts today, many goods now make their way to Iran illicitly that fall below the sanctions list thresholds but are covered by the catch-all condition that bans all goods that could contribute to Iran's nuclear program. The volume of these sales is expected to increase after an agreement takes effect and many more of these goods could get through successfully. **Unless carefully managed, a key risk is that the sanctions may not hold firm for the below threshold or catch-all goods.** Stopping transfers of explicitly banned items may also become more difficult as business opportunities increase and much of the world de-emphasizes Iran's nuclear program as a major issue in their foreign policies and domestic regulations. This could be particularly true for China and middle economic powers, such as Turkey, which already have substantial trade with Iran and are expected to seek expanded ties. Other countries with weak export controls may expand trade as well.

Verified Procurement Channel for Authorized Nuclear Programs

The six powers must carefully plan for these eventualities now and include in any agreement an architecture to mitigate and manage proliferation-related procurement risks. A priority is creating a verifiable procurement channel to route needed goods to Iran's authorized nuclear programs. The agreement will need to allow for imports to legitimate nuclear programs, as they do now for the Bushehr nuclear power reactor.

A challenge will be creating and maintaining an architecture, with a broader nuclear procurement channel, that permits imports of goods to Iran's authorized nuclear programs and possibly later to its civilian industries, while preventing imports to military programs and banned or covert nuclear programs. The UNSC and its Iran sanctions committee and Panel of Experts, the IAEA, and supplier states will all need to play key roles in verifying the end use of exports to Iran's authorized nuclear programs and ensuring that proliferation sensitive goods are not going to banned nuclear activities or military programs.

The creation of the architecture should be accomplished during the negotiations of the long-term deal, although its implementation may need to wait until the long term deal itself is fully implemented. It will be important that the architecture, whether or not implemented later, be established at the very beginning of the implementation of the long-term agreement in order to adequately deal with this issue. In essence, the creation of the architecture should not be left to later.

The reason for creating a verified procurement channel is that Iran's legitimate nuclear activities may need imports. The "modernization" of the Arak reactor would probably involve the most imports, depending on the extent to which international partners are involved. A sensitive area will be any imports, whether equipment, material, or technologies, which are associated with the heavy water portion of the reactor, in the case that the reactor is not converted to light water. Another sensitive set of possible imports involves goods related to the separation of radionuclides from irradiated targets, although goods for reprocessing, i.e. separating plutonium from irradiated fuel or targets, would be banned since Iran is expected to commit in the long-term agreement not to conduct reprocessing. Nonetheless, allowed imports could include goods that would be close in capability to those used in reprocessing, since the boundary in this area between sensitive and non-sensitive equipment is very thin. These goods will therefore require careful monitoring. Iran's centrifuge program, if reduced in scale to the levels required for U.S. acceptance of a deal, will result in a large excess stockpile of key goods for IR-1 centrifuges. This stock should last for many years, eliminating the need for most imports. Nonetheless, the centrifuge program may need certain spare parts, raw materials, or replacement equipment. If Iran continues centrifuge research and development, that program may require sensitive raw materials and equipment. Needless to say, the goods exported to Iran's centrifuge programs will require careful monitoring as to their use and long term fate.

Iran's non-nuclear civilian industries and institutions may also want to purchase dual-use goods covered by the sanctions, but this sector should not expect to be exempted from sanctions during the duration of the deal or at least until late in the deal, Iran must prove it is fully complying with the agreement and will not abuse a civilian sector exemption to obtain banned goods for its nuclear, missile, or other military programs. With renewed economic activity and as part of efforts to expand the high-tech civilian sector, Iranian companies and institutions engaged in civilian, non-nuclear activities can be expected to seek these goods, several of which would be covered by the catch-all condition of the resolutions. Examples of dual-use goods would be carbon fiber, vacuum pumps, valves, computer control equipment, raw materials, subcomponents of equipment, and other proliferation sensitive goods. Currently, these civil industries (Iran's petro-chemical and automotive industries are two such examples) are essentially denied many of these goods under the UNSC resolutions and related unilateral and multilateral sanctions. However, if civilian industries are to be eventually exempted from the sanctions, this exemption must be created with special care, implemented no sooner than many years into the agreement, and monitored especially carefully. Iran could exploit this exemption to obtain goods illicitly for banned activities. It could approach suppliers claiming the goods are for civil purposes but in fact they would be for banned nuclear or military programs. Such a strategy is exactly what Iran's nuclear program has pursued illicitly for many years, including cases where goods were procured under false pretenses by the Iranian oil and gas industry for the nuclear program. There are also many examples of illicit Iranian procurements for its nuclear program where Iranian and other trading companies misrepresented the end use to suppliers.

This architecture covering proliferation sensitive goods should remain in place for the duration of the comprehensive agreement. The six powers must carefully plan for eventualities now and design and implement an architecture that prevents future Iranian illicit procurements under a comprehensive agreement.

3) Render Excess Centrifuges Less Risky

If Iran accepts a sharp limit on the number of centrifuges that would enrich uranium in a comprehensive deal, what about the excess centrifuges? If the limit is about 4,000 IR-1 centrifuges, Iran would need to dismantle or render unusable over 14,000 IR-1 centrifuges and over 1,000 of the more advanced IR-2m centrifuges. These 1,000 IR-2m centrifuges are equivalent of about 3,000-5,000 IR-1 centrifuges. Thus, Iran would need to eliminate a large fraction of its centrifuge program.

The centrifuges in excess of a limit should ideally be destroyed. Failing that, it is critical to ensure that these centrifuges cannot be turned back on in a matter of months. If it can resume operations quickly, Iran could quickly reconstitute its larger enrichment program, and thereby a sizeable breakout capability, if it decided to renege on the deal. Thus, any proposal to keep excess centrifuges installed should be rejected.

Iran's reneging on a cap in centrifuges may happen outside of any overt nuclear weapons breakout. Iran may argue that the United States has not delivered on its commitments and build back up its number of centrifuges in retaliation. By assuaging the international community that it is not breaking out, Iran may make any meaningful U.S. response very difficult.

Some analysts, including those at ISIS, have discussed imposing essentially what have been called in the North Korean context "disablement" steps, which would delay the restart of installed centrifuges. However, ISIS's attempts to define disablement steps that leave the centrifuges and cascade equipment in place appear to be reversible in less than six months of diligent work. This time period applies to proposals to remove the centrifuge pipework from the centrifuge plants.

Moreover, this estimated time for reassembling the centrifuge cascades remains uncertain and it could be shorter. There is no practical experience in disabling centrifuge plants; North Korea's centrifuge program was not subject to disablement. It needs to be pointed out that some U.S. policymakers had a tendency to exaggerate the difficulty of undoing North Korean disablement steps imposed at the Yongbyon nuclear center on plutonium production related facilities. In fact, North Korea was able to reverse several of these steps relatively quickly. A lesson from the North Korean case is that disablement steps are highly reversible and in fact can be reversed faster than expected.

A sounder strategy involves including disablement steps with the destruction of a limited, but carefully selected set of equipment. For example, the deal could include the destruction of certain key cascade equipment, such as valves and pressure or flow measuring equipment. An agreed upon fraction of centrifuges and associated cascade piping and equipment should be kept available under monitored storage away from the centrifuge plants as spares to replace broken centrifuges and equipment. This number would be derived from the current rate of breakage which Iran would need to document with the aid of the IAEA. However, this rate is relatively well known now, as a result of the IAEA's monitoring of Iranian centrifuge manufacturing under the JPA. Iran has provided the IAEA with an inventory of centrifuge rotor assemblies used to replace those centrifuges that have failed, and the IAEA has confirmed that centrifuge rotor manufacturing and assembly have been consistent with Iran's replacement program for damaged centrifuges. Armed with a reliable breakage rate, the negotiators can define the limited stockpile of centrifuges necessary to avoid any Iranian manufacturing of IR-1 centrifuges.

4) Institutionalize a Minimal Centrifuge R&D Program

Another important limit on Iran's nuclear program aims to ensure that an advanced centrifuge R&D program does not become the basis of a surge in capability in case a deal fails or of a covert breakout. Iran's centrifuge research and development (R&D) program poses several risks to the verifiability of a comprehensive deal. Throughout the duration of a long-term comprehensive agreement, Iran's centrifuge R&D program should be limited to centrifuges with capabilities comparable to the current IR-2m centrifuge. The numbers of centrifuges spinning in development cascades should be kept to at most a few cascades.

An open-ended Iranian centrifuge R&D program aimed at developing more sophisticated centrifuges than the IR-2m makes little economic sense. Iran will not be able to produce enriched uranium competitive with that produced by exporting countries such as Russia or URENCO during the next several decades, if ever. Therefore, Iran's investment in a large centrifuge R&D program would be a waste of time and resources. Moreover, the goal of a long-term agreement is to eventually integrate Iran into the international civilian nuclear order (even as a non-exporting producer of enriched uranium). This integration would render mute Iran's claims for self-sufficiency in enriched uranium production or for continuing the program out of national pride.

A long-term agreement should reinforce sound economic principles universally accepted in the world's nuclear programs, all of which are deeply interconnected through an international supply chain based on reactor suppliers and enriched uranium fuel requirements. Building an agreement catering to open-ended, economically unrealistic ambitions is both unnecessary and counterproductive, and also sets dangerous precedents for other potential proliferant states. Iran's development of more advanced centrifuges would also significantly complicate the verification of a long-term agreement. In a breakout or cheating scenario, Iran would need far fewer of these advanced centrifuges in a clandestine plant to make weapon-grade uranium than in one using IR-1 centrifuges. For example, Iran recently claimed it has done initial work on a centrifuge, called the IR-8, reportedly able to produce enriched uranium at a level 16 times greater than the IR-1 centrifuge. Such a centrifuge, if fully developed, would allow Iran to build a centrifuge plant with one sixteenth as many centrifuges. Currently, Iran has about 18,000 IR-1 centrifuges and in a breakout it could produce enough weapon-grade uranium for a nuclear weapon in about two months, according to both U.S. and ISIS estimates. So, instead of needing 18,000 IR-1 centrifuges to achieve this rapid production of weapon-grade uranium, it would need only 1,125 advanced ones to produce as much weapon-grade uranium in the same time. Thus, equipped with more advanced centrifuges Iran would need far fewer centrifuges than if it had to use IR-1 centrifuges, permitting a smaller, easier to hide centrifuge manufacturing complex and far fewer procurements of vital equipment overseas. If Iran made the decision to break out to nuclear weapons, the advanced centrifuges would greatly simplify its ability to build a covert centrifuge plant that would be much harder to detect in a timely manner allowing an international response able to stop Iran from succeeding in building nuclear weapons.

Advanced centrifuges bring with them significant verification challenges that complicate the development of an adequate verification system. Even with an intrusive system that goes beyond the Additional Protocol, IAEA inspectors would be challenged to find such small centrifuge manufacturing sites, detect the relatively few secret procurements from abroad, or find a small, clandestine centrifuge plant outfitted with these advanced centrifuges. Moreover, with such a small plant needing to be built, Iran would also have a far easier time hiding it from Western intelligence agencies.

5) Keep Centrifuge Numbers Below about 2,000-4,000 IR-1 Centrifuges and as a Supplementary Measure Achieve Lower Stocks of LEU Hexafluoride and Oxide

Although an important goal is reducing LEU stocks, their reduction without lowering centrifuge numbers significantly is not a workable proposition. In essence, the priority is lowering centrifuge numbers and strengthening that goal by also reducing the stocks of LEU, whether or not in hexafluoride of oxide forms. Limiting the amount of 3.5 percent LEU hexafluoride to no more than about 500 kilograms appears manageable, as long as the number of IR-1 centrifuges does not exceed roughly 4,000.

As some have proposed, treating these two, reinforcing steps instead as a zero-sum game is counterproductive to achieving an adequate agreement. In this scheme, the number of centrifuges would be raised substantially, to 7,000, 8,000 or more IR-1 centrifuges or equivalent number of advanced ones, while lowering the stocks of 3.5 percent LEU toward zero. In one version of this scheme, only the amount of 3.5 percent LEU hexafluoride would be reduced toward zero via conversion into LEU oxide. Once in oxide form, it would somehow be considered no longer usable in a breakout. But this is wrong. Both chemical forms of LEU have to be considered since Iran can in a matter of months reconvert LEU oxide into hexafluoride form and then feed that material into centrifuges, significantly reducing total breakout time.[6] Iran does not have a way to use large quantities of 3.5 percent LEU in a reactor, so irradiation cannot be counted on to render these oxide stocks unusable. This means that proposals that merely lower the quantity of LEU hexafluoride by converting it into oxide form or fresh fuel is an even more unstable, reversible idea than variants that lower total LEU stocks to zero.

Some background is helpful. This proposal is fundamentally based on Iran not possessing enough 3.5 percent LEU to further enrich and obtain enough weapon-grade uranium (WGU) for a nuclear weapon, taken here as 25 kilograms. If Iran had less than 1,000 kilograms of 3.5 percent LEU hexafluoride, it would not have enough to produce 25 kilograms of WGU. Its breakout time would increase because it would be required to also feed natural uranium into the centrifuges. It could not use the three-step process, where WGU is produced in three steps, with the greatest number of centrifuges taking 3.5 percent to 20 percent LEU, a smaller number enriching from 20 to 60 percent, and a smaller number still going from 60 to 90 percent, or WGU. Instead, Iran would need to add a fourth step at the "bottom" enriching from natural uranium to 3.5 percent LEU. This step would require a large number of centrifuges and thus fewer would be available for the other steps, lengthening breakout times.

Figure 1 shows mean breakout times for a four-step process, where the amount of LEU varies from 0-1000 kilograms of 3.5 percent enriched uranium hexafluoride and each graph represents a fixed number of IR-1 centrifuges, from 4,000 to 18,000. In this case, it is assumed that Iran would have no access to near 20 percent LEU hexafluoride, a dubious assumption (see below). In the figure, a six month breakout time is represented by the black horizontal line on the graph. Several cases are noteworthy. For less than 6,000 IR-1 centrifuges, all of the breakout times exceed six months. For 10,000 IR-1 centrifuges, the breakout time is six months for stocks of 1,000 kilograms of 3.5 percent LEU hexafluoride and exceeds six months for lesser amounts of LEU. For 14,000 centrifuges, when the stock is below about 500 kilograms of 3.5 percent enriched uranium hexafluoride, the breakout time is six months or more. For 18,000 centrifuges, a six month breakout time only occurs for an inventory of zero kilograms of 3.5 percent enriched uranium, a physical impossibility. That number of centrifuges would produce several hundred kilograms of 3.5 percent LEU hexafluoride every month. Much of this material would be in the product tanks hooked to the cascades and thus readily usable. So, cases of no LEU are not achievable.

If instead a one year breakout time was selected, the numbers of centrifuges and LEU stocks would be significantly less. For example, in the unrealistic case of no available near 20 percent LEU, a breakout time of one year would correspond to 6,000 IR-1 centrifuges and a stock of 500 kilograms of 3.5 percent LEU hexafluoride.

In fact, a major weakness in proposals to reduce LEU stocks while keeping centrifuge numbers relatively high is that the very product produced by the centrifuges, namely 3.5 percent LEU, would need to be regularly eliminated through some process. Obtaining this level of compliance would be challenging. Even if the LEU were to be shipped overseas, Iran could hold back sending it abroad, building up a large stock. Similarly, if it were converted into an oxide form, Iran could delay doing so, feigning problems in the conversion plant or delays in transporting it to the plant for conversion. Moreover, conversion to oxide as mentioned above can be rapidly reversed, allowing a three-step process and significantly faster breakout.

In the unlikely case of Iran not mustering any near 20 percent LEU hexafluoride, a plant with 10,000 IR-1 centrifuges would correspond to a six-month breakout limit if the stock did not exceed 1,000 kilograms of 3.5 percent LEU hexafluoride. In two months, however, another five hundred kilograms could be produced in this number of centrifuges, with the total 3.5 percent LEU stock reaching 1,500 kilograms and allowing a three step breakout, which could occur in a matter of a few months. Thus, in practice, LEU stocks would need to be maintained at levels far below 1,000 kilograms, even in the case of 10,000 IR-1 centrifuges. And keeping the stocks below this limit would be very challenging over the duration of a deal. If Iran kept more than 10,000 IR-1 centrifuges, the situation is more untenable.

The above discussion assumes that Iran could not use near 20 percent LEU hexafluoride. Why is this, in fact, unlikely to be the case? Iran has stockpiled relatively large quantities of near 20 percent LEU oxide, quantities way beyond what is necessary to fuel the Tehran Research Reactor. By using this stock, Iran could reduce breakout times considerably after reconverting the near 20 percent LEU oxide into hexafluoride form. Iran currently has enough near 20 percent LEU, if reconverted into hexafluoride form and further enriched, to yield enough weapon-grade uranium for a nuclear weapon. The comprehensive agreement should certainly further reduce the size of the near 20 percent LEU stock; however, Iran is not expected to eliminate this stock, as long as Iran will fuel the Tehran Research Reactor (TRR). In the future, Iran could start to reconvert this material to hexafluoride form in a matter of months and dramatically speed up breakout.

Figure 2 shows the impact of only 50 kilograms of near 20 percent LEU hexafluoride on mean breakout times, where again a four-step process is used. With just 50 kilograms of near 20 percent LEU hexafluoride, a stock of 500 kilograms of 3.5 percent LEU hexafluoride, and 10,000 IR-1 centrifuges, breakout time would be six months. For comparison, in the case of no near 20 percent LEU discussed above, 10,000 IR-1 centrifuges could achieve a six-month breakout only with a stock of 1,000 kilograms of 3.5 percent LEU hexafluoride. So, 50 kilograms of near 20 percent LEU hexafluoride is equivalent to roughly 500 kilograms of 3.5 percent LEU hexafluoride. If a stock of 50 kilograms of near 20 percent LEU hexafluoride is used in conjunction with a stock of 1,000 kilograms of 3.5 percent LEU hexafluoride, Iran would have enough LEU hexafluoride to use a three-step process to break out and achieve breakout times of a few months.

So, in a realistic case whereby Iran would need to accumulate only 50 kilograms of near 20 percent LEU hexafluoride, a six month breakout would correspond to 10,000 IR-1 centrifuges and a stock of 3.5 percent LEU that could not exceed 500 kilograms. While in theory this limit could be maintained, in practice that is highly unlikely. Each month, such a plant would produce almost 250 kilograms of 3.5 percent LEU hexafluoride. In two months, Iran could exceed the cap by 500 kilograms, reaching a total of 1,000 kilograms of 3.5 percent LEU hexafluoride, or enough if used in combination with the near 20 percent LEU hexafluoride stock to reduce breakout times to about four months, all the while claiming that some reasonable problems prevent it from removing the excess material.

If instead a one year breakout time was selected, the numbers of centrifuges and LEU stocks would again be significantly less. For example, a breakout time of one year would correspond to 6,000 IR-1 centrifuges and a stock of about 200 kilograms of 3.5 percent LEU hexafluoride. In the case of 4,000 IR-1 centrifuges, the breakout time would be about 12 months with about 700 kilograms of 3.5 percent LEU hexafluoride. If the LEU limit was set at about 500 kilograms of 3.5 percent hexafluoride, and given that a limit could easily be exceeded by a few hundred kilograms, the numbers of IR-1 centrifuges should not exceed 4,000.

In sum, lowering stocks in support of the fundamental goal of sharply limiting centrifuge numbers is a useful measure that would strengthen a deal. If stockpile limits are exceeded, that violation would pose minimal risk to the agreement as long as the centrifuge numbers are small.

6) Beware the concept of "SWU" as a Limit

Enrichment effort is measured in separative work units (SWU). However, setting limits on the annual SWU of a centrifuge plant has several problems. One is that determining the annual SWU of a centrifuge plant is difficult and its average value can change. Iran for example suggested in the negotiations that it would be willing to reduce the speed of its centrifuges and the amount of natural uranium fed into the centrifuge cascades, while it kept the same number of centrifuges. Both of these measures would reduce the annual SWU of the centrifuge plants, potentially significantly, even reduce it by a third of its existing enrichment output. But in a day, Iran could reduce these steps and reclaim its original enrichment capability; it is easy to increase the speed and the feed rate. Not surprisingly, Western negotiators soundly rejected this proposal.

While SWU has a role to play in determining the equivalence of different types of centrifuges, it should not be a limit in its own right.

7) Ensure the Arak Reactor's Changes are Irreversible

Iran appears to accept that it must limit plutonium production in the heavy water Arak nuclear reactor (IR-40), which is almost 90 percent complete and under a construction moratorium because of the interim nuclear deal. As presently designed, the reactor can be used relatively easily to make weapon-grade plutonium, at a production rate of up to about nine kilograms a year. This plutonium could later be separated and used in nuclear weapons.

Strategies for lowering plutonium production have been discussed publicly, where the reactor would use five percent enriched uranium fuel instead of natural uranium fuel and its power would be reduced by more than half, from 40 megawatts-thermal (MWth) to 10-20 MWth. This strategy would involve placing LEU fuel in a small fraction of the fuel channels in a. large vessel – often called a "calandria"—through which the heavy water moderator and coolant flows. The Arak calandria has about 175 fuel and control rod channels. The LEU would be inserted into the middle section of the calandria with the majority of channels left empty. There are two problems remaining in this strategy, namely whether the calandria would be replaced with one sized for LEU fuel and the heat exchangers would be downsized appropriately to those needed for a 10-20 MWth reactor.

Although the outcomes of reduced power and enriched uranium fuel are preferred, leaving Iran with an unmodified Arak calandria and its original heat exchangers constitutes an unacceptable proposal. If the core and heat exchangers were left intact, Iran could in a straightforward manner switch back to a natural uranium core and 40 MWth of power, undoing this limitation on plutonium production. This reconversion could occur in the open and under IAEA safeguards where Iran creates some pretext. In terms of the natural uranium fuel, Iran has already made significant progress on preparing a core load of natural uranium fuel, which could be finished, or the experience used to fabricate another one. Once switched back, Iran could run the reactor under safeguards to produce plutonium, even weapon-grade plutonium. Since the reactor would be fully operational, its destruction via military means would be dangerous and highly risky, and on balance unlikely to occur. Then, at the time of its choosing, Iran could breakout, having only to separate the plutonium from the spent fuel, which could be done utilizing a covert, low technology reprocessing plant in a matter of a few months. The designs for this type of plant are unclassified and readily available and such a plant would be very difficult for the IAEA (or intelligence agencies) to detect either during its relatively short construction or subsequent operation.

At a minimum, Iran should remove the existing calandria and replace it with one sized appropriately for a core of the agreed upon number of LEU fuel assemblies. The existing one should be rendered unusable or removed from Iran.

Despite the merits of modifying the Arak reactor, a more effective compromise remains upgrading the Arak reactor to a modern light water research reactor (LWR) which can be designed to be far more capable of making medical isotopes than the current Arak reactor design. It can also be designed to make plutonium production in targets much more difficult to accomplish than the Arak reactor or older style research reactors.

A proposal to do so involves ensuring that the LWR is built irreversibly with a power of 10 MWth. This would require remanufacturing of the Arak reactor and changes to the heat exchangers and cooling system. Under this proposal, there is no need to produce heavy water, and the current stocks could be sold on the world market. Production of natural uranium oxide powder, fuel pellets, rods, and assemblies for the Arak IR-40 would be halted. Moreover, the associated process lines would also need to be shut-down, including the production of specifically IR-40 relevant materials such as zirconium tubes. In return, the P5+1 could assist Iran in producing fuel for the LWR. Iran could produce the necessary LEU in its enrichment program.

Figure 1: Four Step Enrichment Predictions with no near 20 Percent LEU
Breakout Time Calculation (includes 2 week setup time)
4000, 6000, 10000, 14000, 18000 IR-1 Centrifuges
Range of 3.5% Inventory Used, 0-1000 kg UF$_6$

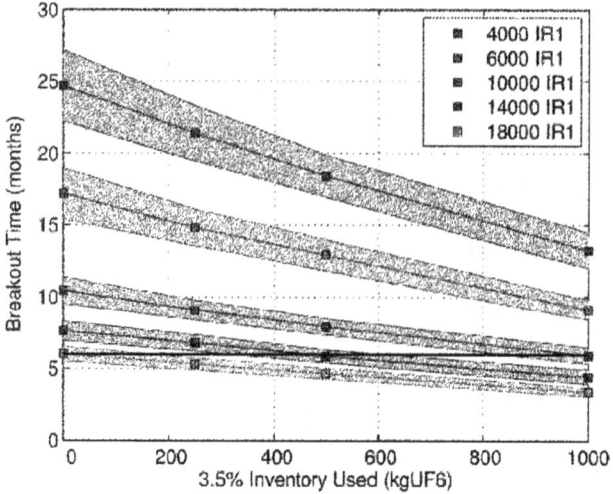

Mean (with range) breakout time versus 3.5% inventory used

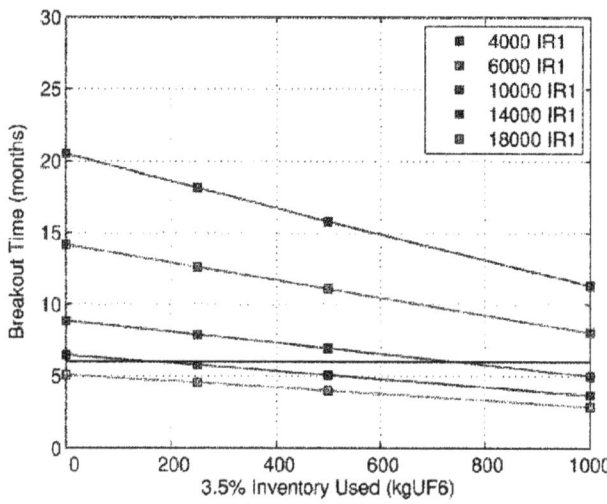

Minimum breakout time versus 3.5% inventory used.

Note: The results are calculated as breakout times for various numbers of centrifuges and amounts of 3.5% inventory used, with multiple scenarios for each number of centrifuges matched with a specific 3.5% inventory. Two sets of breakout times are reported in the figures mean with range and minimum value of all scenarios. The results in the text use the mean values. The minimum values are viewed as worst case estimates which may be unlikely to be achieved in practice.

Figure 2: Four Step Enrichment Estimate with 50 kg near 20 percent LEUF$_6$ Used
Breakout Time Calculation (includes 2 week setup time)
4000, 6000, 10000, 14000, 18000 IR-1 Centrifuges
Range of 3.5% Inventory Used: 0-1000 kg LEUF$_6$

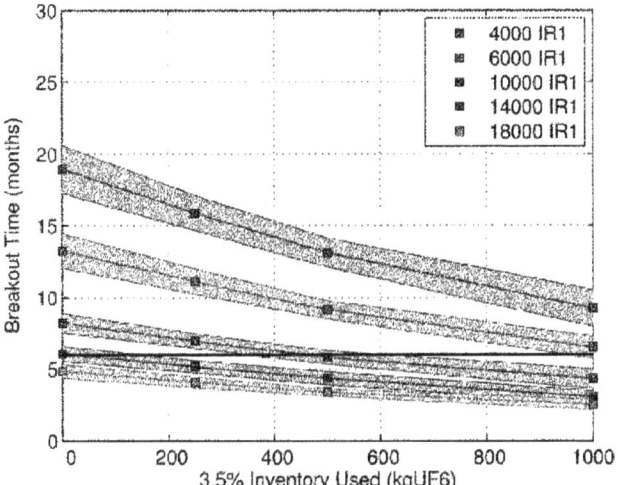

Mean (with range) breakout time versus 3.5% inventory used

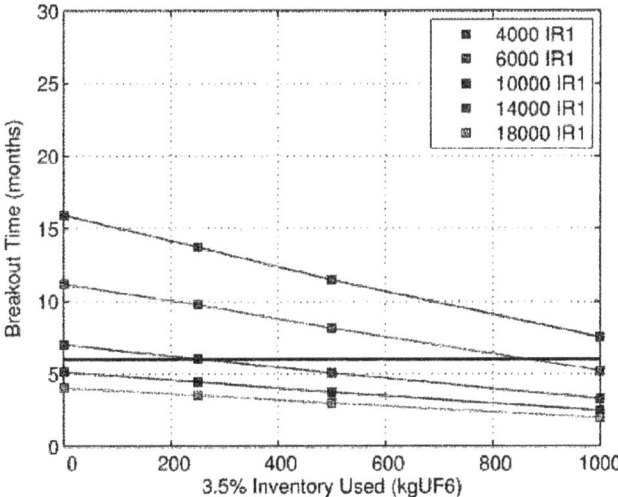

Minimum breakout time versus 3.5% inventory used

Note: The results are calculated as breakout times for various numbers of centrifuges and amounts of 3.5% inventory used, with multiple scenarios for each number of centrifuges matched with a specific 3.5% inventory. Two sets of breakout times are reported in the figures: mean with range and minimum value of all scenarios. The results in the text use the mean values. The minimum values are viewed as worst case estimates which may be unlikely to be achieved in practice.

Mr. POE. Thank you, gentlemen. The Chair will begin with its questions—5 minutes of questions.

Are the Iranians working on a delivery system for nuclear weapons—intercontinental ballistic missiles?

Mr. MCINNIS. I would say that the pursuit of an ICBM has been something that the Iranian regime has been going after for some time. I think the U.S. intelligence community has been watching that fairly closely.

So, obviously, they portray it as usually tied to their space program or other types of activities but

Mr. POE. The Iranians have a space program?

Mr. MCINNIS. They have been able to put some stuff up there.

Mr. POE. I understand. But the intercontinental ballistic missile pursuit that is not a part of the negotiations and this discussion, as far as I know. Is that correct?

Mr. ALBRIGHT. Yes. No, the missiles are not. That is one of the reasons why you want to keep the U.N. Security Council sanctions in place because one would expect them to go out and acquire or seek goods illicitly.

Now, the reentry vehicle that would hold a nuclear weapon and the warhead itself are certainly part of this and a lot of the IAEA's concerns are exactly on those two issues. In 2003, their information is that they were developing a reentry vehicle and developing a warhead that was about .55 meters across that could fit inside that reentry vehicle. So that part of it is very much part of this issue.

Mr. POE. Are the Iranians delaying and cheating at the same time, in your opinion? Delaying implementation of another deal but also pursuing violations of previous agreements. What is your opinion on that?

Mr. MCINNIS. I mean, would you characterize the IR–5 issue that has come up as a——

Mr. ALBRIGHT. Yes, we asked the question if the IR–5 or feeding the IR–5 was a violation. I mean, we think it shouldn't have happened. I mean, we are not lawyers so I would go as far as saying we think it shouldn't have happened.

Now, the issue of violation. Right now the IAEA says that Iran's declared program is in compliance with its obligations under the nonproliferation treaty.

They cannot say if there are undeclared nuclear activities or facilities that Iran may be pursuing. They don't have the mechanisms and the tools to do that. So we just don't know.

On the PMD, the IAEA continues to say that some of the activities, and they would talk about nuclear weapons-related activities, may have continued and I don't know if that would be a violation but it would certainly be troubling if that was the case.

Mr. TAKEYH. I just——

Mr. POE. Sure.

Mr. TAKEYH. I think there are six U.N. resolutions—Security Council resolutions—including 1929 that was negotiated in May 2010 that have enjoined Iran to suspend all its enrichment and reprocessing activities.

And so the continuation of those activities stand in violation of that. So in a sense, the entirety of the Iranian program that continues to operate is an illicit one.

Mr. POE. Mr. McInnis, do you want to weigh in that?

Mr. MCINNIS. No. I certainly don't disagree with Dr. Takeyh's assessment on that.

Mr. POE. You do disagree or do not?

Mr. MCINNIS. No, I definitely do not disagree with it. What I would add is, certainly, given the history of Iran's nuclear program, in my own personal opinion, I would be very, very surprised if there is not some type of clandestine and other types of activities ongoing that we, obviously, don't know about or it is going to be a while before we find out.

So that is, again, there is nothing in their history to change that assessment.

Mr. POE. Has the supreme leader's statements, philosophy about demanding the destruction of Israel and then the destruction of the United States, has that changed his political statements?

Mr. TAKEYH. No. Actually, he has remained rather persistent in his notion and kind of fantastic claims that he attributes to the United States such as, for instance, that the United States deployed atomic weapons in Japan to test them out against—to see how it would work on human beings. I mean, he makes—those statements continue unabated. So he is not providing his nuclear negotiators with sufficient public relations concessions.

Mr. POE. And I agree with you. He has not changed their philosophy about destruction of Israel and the United States and we ought to deal with them with that understanding.

The Chair will yield 5 minutes to the ranking member, Mr. Sherman from California, for his opening or his questions.

Mr. SHERMAN. Thank you. We ought to be trying to prevent them from developing missiles but let us remember you can smuggle a nuclear weapon. It is about the size of a person.

If Iran were to smuggle one into an American city and then let us know they had it somewhere there, that would put them in a position to blackmail us. Or if they decided to use a nuclear weapon against the United States they could do so with plausible deniability and I don't know how you would have retaliation in the absence of being sure that you knew where the weapon came from.

Among all the things we are doing for Iran or at least in ways that benefit them our Sunni allies and human rights groups have asked us for a no-fly zone. That might very well lead to the departure of Assad, but we have not done so, just one of the many forbearances that Iran benefits from. I don't want to get partisan here but I noticed one of my colleagues talking about the collapse of our foreign policy under this administration. That implies that there was a foreign policy against Iran with the prior administration. I will simply say that most of you think this is genuine male pattern baldness.

It is actually what happens to a Member of Congress who spends 8 years pounding my head into a very effective and successful Bush administration that was successful in not enforcing a single one of our sanctions and not allowing Congress to pass a single significant statutory sanction in 8 years.

The question is what is to be done. We are going to need additional sanctions on Iran unless we get a good agreement and we are not going to get a good agreement if we don't have the prospect of much tougher sanctions, regime-threatening sanctions.

I have got two ideas I want to preview with our panel but, more importantly, I want to get your ideas because our negotiators will not be successful unless Iran is convinced that their economy will be crippled in 2015 by actions taken in the United States Congress should they fail to reach a deal with the United States.

One of those ideas is to take all the way down to zero in a 3-month period the amount of oil that we allow countries to buy and still be able to transact business with the New York Fed and dollar U-turn transactions.

We listened to our allies who said, don't eliminate all of our access to Iranian oil—there might be an oil shortage and what will that do to our economy.

The world is currently swimming in oil. Some of my colleagues are concerned that oil is selling too low and that that is having an averse effect. I don't join them in that pain.

But, certainly, our allies can deal with $75 a barrel oil. Second, we could provide that—so as to cut Iran off from all the major Western and Japanese multinational corporations that if any corporation—has any contract with the United States Government that it must certify that all of its parent and subsidiary and brother-sister corporations are adhering to U.S. sanctions against Iran, which I describe as the not one paper clip rule, so that we would put Iran in a position where it could not do business with any of the world's major multinational groups or corporations.

I would like our—I will start with you, Doctor, both to comment on those but to give me some other ideas. What would cause at least a little bit of fear in Qom right now?

Mr. TAKEYH. The Iranian Central Bank has suggested, for what it is worth and it is usually not worth very much, that what they need for their budgetary allocations about oil to be about $70.

So any kind of reduction——

Mr. SHERMAN. Oh, clearly, the best sanctions didn't come from our committee. The best sanctions came from lowering the price of oil from $140 down to below $75.

Mr. TAKEYH. So anything below that, if that figure is taken into consideration, will likely to affect it. To have the kind of sanctions regarding cutting off Iran along the pace that you are suggesting, I think that has to be accompanied by very significant diplomacy with our allies and China and other countries.

In and of itself, I think it is going to create some disquiet in those particular capitals and it is going to lead to a lot of complaints. I think with suitable diplomacy and a lot of work it might come about.

My suggestion has always been in terms of congressional action. A lot of people are involved in dealing with the Iranian nuclear negotiations—5+1, U.S. and so on.

Mr. SHERMAN. I have got to go. I have got to go on to your co-panelists here.

Mr. TAKEYH. I think you should have the parameters of what is an acceptable deal legislated.

Mr. SHERMAN. Yes?

Mr. MCINNIS. I would just add to Dr. Takeyh Rouhani's economic reforms, which are actually part of what has been going on behind the scenes here, I mean, Ray is right in that they need about, you know, $70, $75 to be able to maintain their current budget.

But for the kinds of structural reforms that Rouhani needs to get the economy moving past the really horrible management of Ahmadinejad for the previous 8 years, he needs more money than $70, $75.

So that is one of the reasons why I think the oil is having a major impact on their calculus right now. Certainly, on being able to cut them off from finances and money to the greatest degree that you can do toward that is always going to be the, you know, that plus oil prices is the—is the right combination, from my perspective.

Mr. ALBRIGHT. Yes. We don't work on sanctions but I think what we see in my group is there is a need for a Plan B, as we have called it. Ideally, that Plan B would be run by the administration, if things are not going to work out. I don't think we have reached that point. I don't think we will reach it in November if there is an extension, that there is a need to be able to impose sanctions and to be able to modulate those sanctions.

And so I think, from my own point of view, the best situation would be if the administration and Congress are working together to create a Plan B.

Now, I understand your frustration. There isn't exactly that kind of cooperation going on and so——

Mr. SHERMAN. We will get to the administration panel next and its presence here demonstrates how closely they are working with us.

Mr. ALBRIGHT. Okay. And so I think it if this isn't going to work, I think the planning for the additional sanctions has to be going on now because you also, and I would want to recommend the administration do this, you don't want to have it happen in 1 day—in 1 day.

Mr. POE. Excuse me, Mr. Albright. Time has expired. Time has expired.

Mr. ALBRIGHT. Okay.

Mr. POE. Excuse me. The Chair will recognize the gentleman from South Carolina, Mr. Wilson, for 5 minutes for his questions.

Mr. WILSON. Thank you, Judge Poe, for your leadership in conducting this hearing. I am very grateful that in my home state of South Carolina we have a significant number of Iranian Americans who are leaders in our state in the medical community and business community.

It is a very dynamic community that means a lot for our state, and I meet with so many of them who are in distress about the authoritarian regime in Tehran and how sad it is that the young people of Iran are held back because of the regime there and denied freedom and democracy, which can be so positive for such a great culture as that of Iran.

Mr. McInnis, a very important question which is facing Congress is what should be the minimum requirements that Iran should meet before Congress agrees to lift the major sanctions that it has imposed?

Included in the question is the future of Iranian enrichment the Arak heavy water reactor, answering questions about the possible military dimensions and past Iranian violations of the United Nations sanctions, the underground Fordow fuel enrichment plant and Iran's nuclear-capable missile force?

Mr. MCINNIS. I mean, the short answer should be all of those but, certainly, if we are going to be looking at lifting the sanctions and, again, I want to emphasize and from my comments and my submitted testimony that, you know, we have to be careful about what is tied in with human rights violations and counterterrorism sanctions in with the nuclear sanctions.

Not that they were necessarily all tied together to begin with, but some of these same mechanisms that we use, you know, so far as financial sanctions have a compounding effect on the situation.

For me, I mean, it is coming clean on the PMD and being able to cap the ability for their enrichment to a breakout level. We talked about the breakout idea. Six to 12 months, for me, is a minimum—that we have to have that type of warning to be able to do something and we need to be—do whatever we can to prevent whatever clandestine or covert activities are happening right now.

Mr. WILSON. Thank you very much, and Dr. Takeyh, how do we trust a regime that has doubled executions of its own people, called explicitly, as you have indicated, for the destruction of another U.N. member, being the state of Israel, labels the United States the Great Satan, exports terrorism as a matter of state policy and has trained and supplied terrorists, including the IEDs that we faced in Iraq which have killed U.S. soldiers?

And how can we trust them to abide by any agreement?

Mr. TAKEYH. I think it would be very difficult and I suspect in any agreement as even in JPOA there will be occasions and indications of violations. There are two things I will say.

Any agreement negotiated with Iran, as I think Dave has suggested, has to have clarification of previous military activities. I don't know if you can actually verify a current agreement without knowing the clandestine history of the program.

Second of all, I will say U.N. Security Council resolutions should be suspended in the event of a deal and not discarded because then you have a mechanism that can come online should there be indication of Iranian violation.

Mr. WILSON. Thank you very much. And, Mr. McInnis, out of what has been leaked and/or disclosed about a potential final deal, what most concerns you?

Mr. MCINNIS. For me, it is that we are not going to be able to resolve the PMD issues and that, frankly, that we are not going to be able to really have an effective metric and mechanism to monitor the enrichment capacities.

So those and, certainly, the other sidebar issue of whether this is going to lead into other efforts we may do with them regarding ISIS, and other things that I fear very much where the path that we are going down, we are being a little naive about that.

Mr. WILSON. Thank you very much and I yield the balance of my time.

Mr. POE. The Chair recognizes the gentleman from California, Mr. Lowenthal, for 5 minutes.

Mr. LOWENTHAL. Thank you, Mr. Chair. I am just trying to understand kind of where we are now and where we go to follow up, I guess, on some of the questions raised by Congressman Sherman.

As I understand, we are not going to have an agreement. We will probably be talking about an extension after the 24th of November. I am also hearing that both Iran, for different reasons, and the United States it would be beneficial to both to have some kind of agreement for different reasons and that—and I am wondering, and I thought I heard also that a stalemate in these negotiations will benefit the United States more than Iran.

Is that true or not, and why is that so and how long does that mean, given the existing conditions that we have?

Mr. TAKEYH. In terms of extension of an agreement, November 24th is a sort of a self-declared deadline. They actually—according to the terms of JPOA, they have until January so that date is in many ways a self-imposed deadline.

I think the Iranian regime, given its predicament, probably requires an agreement more than 5+1 do simply because they arouse expectations of the population that they are going to get financial relief and somehow their economic fortunes are going to turn, and you really cannot have a normal economy in Iran in absence of a nuclear agreement because so much of its economic activities are retarded by international sanctions, banking regulations and so on.

So we do have that leverage going forward that the Iranian regime is in a worse position than we are.

Mr. LOWENTHAL. Do you all agree with that?

Mr. McINNIS. I, certainly, would agree with that and I pointed out in my initial comments that we are in a situation where we have underestimated, in my opinion, our leverage. And, as was also pointed out by the chair and the ranking member, we are actually in a situation of bringing them to the table but in many ways the effects of these sanctions were not really allowed to settle.

I mean, we could have gone much further by keeping up these sanctions at their current pace because the impact that was happening on their reduction in GDP, their inflation issues, those are very serious and, again, as I pointed out before, it wasn't just their current economy.

They have very long-term problems that in some ways have nothing to do with the sanctions. But they can't solve those problems without having major infusions of cash and better access to the international markets.

Mr. ALBRIGHT. Yes. I guess on a technical level and then on a sanctions level I am not sure I agree. I mean, I think in the short run I think we have a tremendous advantage.

But they continue to operate centrifuges. They are learning to operate them better. They are working on more advanced centrifuges in places that are outside the purview of the International Atomic Energy Agency.

The way they have structured their centrifuge R & D program the IAEA does not know how well they are working even at the places where they are monitoring.

And so I think they are going to make progress and that is worrisome in the long run. The other is that, again, I am not a sanctions expert but I can look and see in the news from places like Germany the exports to Iran are increasing.

You know, there are things happening. It is just, you know, people are getting used to it. They are being more relaxed about it. I mean, we continue at ISIS to see Iran actively going out to buy things illegally for its nuclear program.

We see in the last couple years that they have actually become more sophisticated at hiding, particularly, the connection between the nuclear program in Iran and the trading companies that go out and get these things and that is important because you can't chase everything.

So if you had information linking the effort to the nuclear program then you would apply more resources. So I think that in the long run I am not so sure, I think, that this plays best for us.

Mr. LOWENTHAL. Thank you, and I yield back.

Mr. POE. I thank the gentleman. The Chair recognizes Mr. Kinzinger from Illinois for 5 minutes and his questions.

Mr. KINZINGER. Close. Close. Thank you. Thank you, Mr. Chairman, and thank you all for being here. I will say to the ranking member and, with a bit of a smile, I get your point about the collapse of foreign policy.

I wasn't speaking of just Iran. I was more thinking of the rest of the world and everywhere else. So but let me just say thank you all for being here.

As I mentioned in my opening statement, with Iraq specifically, again, and I want to make this mention one more time, as Mr. Wilson alluded to as well, there are American soldiers that are not alive today because of the actions of Iran.

I think that is something that is very important to keep in mind. Not just direct Iranian involvement, which existed—I know that first hand as a veteran of the area—but also with the supplying of materiel and knowledge meant to kill American soldiers, meant to take their lives away because of their meddling in the region, which they have been doing everywhere.

We see Iran very vested in propping up Bashar al-Assad in Syria, investing financial resources in this, by the way. At a time when supposedly their economy is so bad even in the interim deal that they are, you know, going to do whatever the United States wants, they are investing in the existence of this guy who has brutally murdered 200,000 of his own people—Bashar al-Assad.

Keep in mind, I know ISIS is a major concern. We are all united on that. But the existence of Assad is an anathema to humanity, in my mind, and the way he governs.

I just want to ask the three of you a couple of questions. First off, what message do you think was sent to Iran in terms of helping them to come to an agreement that makes sense for us and for the peaceful world?

What message was sent? You know, what we are seeing today in Russia, for instance? Iran doesn't just look at the Middle East. They look at the United States foreign policy all over the place. The Iraq pullout in 2011 as well as the comments by the administration about this idea of a pivot away from the Middle East, which I know and I have heard from the administration they regret using those words and I understand that and I appreciate it.

But they were used and that is the perception. So I ask the three of you if you could talk about kind of those foreign policy areas where, I think, there has been some difficulty and talk about what message that has sent to Iran in terms of motivating them to come to the table with a good deal for us.

Mr. TAKEYH. On the issue of the tensions between United States and the Russian Federation, I think they have become more obvious and a more tangible impact on the negotiations if there is a breakdown of some sort of a diplomacy on the P5+1.

I think then you can see the Russians pulling away from the 5+1 consensus as may the Chinese as well in terms of repatriating Iranian money and so on. So the Russian angle is not obvious at this point but it can be.

The region itself today is, as you mentioned, Congressman, is rather disorderly, to say the least, and Iran is an opportunistic country that is trying to take advantage in Syria, in Iraq, in Lebanon, in Yemen, and so they do seem to be engaged in a sort of a cold war with the Saudis that is playing us off throughout the region.

And as I have mentioned, there is a persistent narrative on the Iranian leadership that, you know, they do have opportunities at this point that they have to exploit because they were not that obvious before.

Mr. KINZINGER. But wouldn't it—it also seems that if we had Iran, and I think we did a year ago, to the point where they were in pretty—I mean, we had our boots on their neck, basically, on these—or before the negotiations started.

But if even in this interim agreement is such that, you know, their economy is still taking it on the chin, they have been able to invest a stunning amount of resources in expanding their influence around the Middle East. It has been amazing.

Mr. TAKEYH. There is no question that they are apportioning whatever money they have in an injudicious way and the welfare of their population doesn't seem to be their priority on that. That is true about most revolutionary states and this is one of them.

Mr. MCINNIS. I would just add to that point that one of our major foreign policy failures several years ago was the underestimation of how far Iran would go to prop up Assad.

I think there was a general consensus here in Washington and other capitals that Assad's days were numbered, as the President said. That really underestimated the fact that Syria is absolutely essential for Iran's foreign policy, for its ideological objectives, for its religious objectives, that they cannot—even if they have lots of problems with Assad himself, they can't lose Syria and I think we have kind of lost the fact that Iran is not going to be pulling back from its foreign policies that it has been pursuing since the end of their revolution.

And, frankly, on the money issue, yeah, the money keeps flowing but at the same time the amount of money it needs—that Iran needs to be able to kind of keep up its efforts there in the region is still—I mean, Iran—as much as Iran's economy is strained, it still doesn't spend tons of money on military issues. Its percentage of GDP on defense is, like, under 4 percent.

Mr. KINZINGER. And because my time is up, I just want to wrap up with saying this. I think if there is an attempt by the administration to come to this body and even—or not come to the body but say, we need additional time, I mean, I hope and I think there would be bipartisan support to not give that because I can't see what would happen in another 6 months that we didn't have an opportunity to do in the first year and I, frankly, think reinstating the sanctions and walking away from the table and saying fine, you chose your own destiny, is much more powerful than saying yeah, I know, we didn't have enough conversations so you need another 6 months. I yield back.

Mr. POE. The gentleman yields back his time. The Chair recognizes Mr. Schneider, the gentleman from Illinois.

Mr. SCHNEIDER. Thank you, Mr. Chairman.

Dr. Takeyh, you mentioned that there are multiple—you referenced the fact that there are multiple U.N. Security Council resolutions saying that Iran has effectively zero right to enrichment.

Yet, Mr. Albright, you talked about, potentially, 4,000 centrifuges. Could all of you touch on, I'm trying to think of the best way to phrase the question is why, if any, number of centrifuges are acceptable for a final agreement with Iran?

Mr. TAKEYH. I think the U.N. Security Council resolutions have suggested that Iran has to suspend its activities and come into compliance and then a deal can be negotiated that may actually involve some residual enrichment.

One of the assumptions that has guided the United States across two administrations has been that, if you settle for limited number of centrifuges and limited enrichment, then Iranian pride would be satisfied and therefore they would settle for that permanent symbolic program.

What the Iranians have said persistently, publicly and privately, is that they are seeking an industrial-size program. So whatever enrichment capacity they have, they do envision that capacity to be industrialized, and I would just say that the comprehensive deal that is being negotiated today in of itself is also an interim deal of duration.

It will have a sunset clause at some point. Maybe that sunset clause is 15 years, maybe it is 10 years, and there is some discrepancy about that. But subsequent to that, Iran is under no legal stricture to expand its program.

It can, therefore, have an industrial enrichment capability that is legal, sanctioned and without any hazards of economic penalties.

Mr. SCHNEIDER. Mr. McInnis?

Mr. MCINNIS. Actually, I yield to Mr. Albright.

Mr. ALBRIGHT. Yes. If you think of it in terms of breakout time, which is what drove us to this number and it is a combination of centrifuges and stocks——

Mr. SCHNEIDER. Yes, I have turned in your submitted testimony to the charts.

Mr. ALBRIGHT. Okay. Oh, okay. But if they had no centrifuges at all we would estimate their breakout time is 2 years. So, they know how to do it. They can make them and so you can't eliminate that and so then the question is how many can you accept under some kind of criteria like breakout and verifiability and we ended up that we could live with 4,000.

Now, in terms of their right, I think we're paying a very heavy price. I mean, I am not a lawyer. I understand—I have seen Senator Kerry say they have no right to enrich—it is not in the treaty.

But for us, it is a tough compromise to accept because we work just as much on North Korea, in theory at least, as Iran. This is a special time, and that pivot to Asia, while it may be opposed by those working on the Middle East, those working on North Korea see a desperate need for more U.S. attention to stop North Korea's nuclear weapons advancements.

And so, now I know it probably will be impossible to argue that North Korea give up its centrifuge program because of what is happening in Iran.

So I think that it is where compromises are being made. We are accepting them at my organization but they are very problematic and they are going to cause problems and that means that, in any deal that is gained, Iran has to be made to pay a very heavy price for it and there does need to be some kind of condition at the end so that the program is under special arrangements that keep it and other countries from being able to claim that they can just go ahead and build as many centrifuges as they want.

Mr. SCHNEIDER. And—I am sorry. Go ahead, Mr. McInnis.

Mr. MCINNIS. I would just add one quick comment on that. One of the things I think we underestimated in why Iran came to the table last year is because, as Mr. Albright was saying, they have actually achieved a certain technological capability that is almost impossible to walk backwards from and so that is something that, you know, once they had—which they were not at, say, 6, 7 years ago when there was much more at risk for them.

So I think they are at a confidence level that allows them to come to the table because there is only so much we can do to them.

Mr. SCHNEIDER. Thank you. Mr. Albright, to build on your comment, at zero centrifuges because of their know-how they are 2 years away from a breakout.

At the current 19,000, approximately, IR–1 centrifuges if they were to operate all of those you estimated a year ago that the JPOA moved it back from, if I remember correctly, 1.3 to 1.6 months?

Mr. ALBRIGHT. Yes, there is a difference now for us. It was from 2 months to 3 months, that was the walk back, still well within 20 percent.

Mr. SCHNEIDER. But still well within a year. My question is what is an acceptable time frame moving them back from that 3 months to somewhere between 3 months and 2 years that the international community should be expected to live with if there is a number?

Mr. ALBRIGHT. The U.S. position is 1 year. That translates into, at least in our calculations, about 2,000 IR–1s staying in place with certain amounts of low-enriched uranium.

So we think 6 months and, again, it is 6 months to the point where they have enough weapon-grade uranium for a bomb and we think that is—that is acceptable.

The administration told us many times that they want a year. They see ours as too short and, you know, if they can get a year I am all for it.

Mr. SCHNEIDER. Just because of limited time I am going to take back and turn now to the Iraq heavy water reactor. Is there——

Mr. POE. The gentleman's time has expired.

Mr. SCHNEIDER. I am out of time.

Mr. POE. The Chair recognizes the gentleman from Pennsylvania, Mr. Perry, for 5 minutes.

Mr. PERRY. Thank you, Mr. Chairman. Thank you, gentlemen. It seems to me that any negotiation deal is predicated on trust and whether it is regarding Iran's nuclear program or buying a car that is the minimum requirement.

So with that in mind, as far as I am aware, last month the IAEA reported that Iran did not provide information about work it had completed on high explosives for a nuclear bomb and other possible military dimensions of its nuclear program, even though it promised to do so back in November 2011.

So we're 3 years in. Can anybody explain what this means? I mean, to me it is somewhat obvious but maybe I am missing something.

Sometimes things are counterintuitive. So is there something I am—you know, if I am trying to build a nuclear weapon I imagine I want a triggering device and so on and so forth and I don't want to tell anybody if everybody is mad about me doing it.

So this seems axiomatic to me. Are we foolish Americans missing something?

Mr. ALBRIGHT. No, I don't think so. No, I think it is one of the reasons why I don't think there should be a deal until Iran has demonstrated some concrete progress on addressing the inspectors' issues and that dealing with the high explosives was one of the test cases.

They promised to do it I forget when. Was it back in May, I think? And they didn't and then they told the IAEA, in my mind making it even worse, that we don't even want to have another meeting until after November 24th.

So I think it is a very troubling development and I think what Iran is trying to do is seeing if they can get away with it. There are also many people who are saying the past doesn't matter and that why do we bother with this.

So I think it is very important that Congress have a very strong voice in saying that it does matter and I know all my experience in inspections and working on verification is the past does matter and the warning for that should be what happened in Iraq in 1991 when the IAEA and others did not worry about the past and only focused on the present and the future. It turned out they had a very large nuclear weapons program that had been missed by the inspectors.

So I think the IAEA learned from that and they want to know the past.

Mr. PERRY. Well, why wouldn't the past matter in this context? I mean, what other measure of trust would you have? If you just met somebody—Country A met Country B for the first time—you establish a certain level—a base level of trustworthiness because you have to start somewhere.

But in this context——

Mr. ALBRIGHT. Well, you can't build it on trust. That is why they have the rules we want to know the past.

Mr. PERRY. Right.

Mr. ALBRIGHT. I mean, you can't build it on trust. Maybe you can—later you can have trust——

Mr. PERRY. But aren't our—but aren't our actions currently—don't they portend that they are built on trust?

Mr. ALBRIGHT. No, I—no, I don't think so. No, I don't——

Mr. PERRY. Are our actions?

Mr. ALBRIGHT. In terms of there is—in the negotiations I think there has been quite a rapport built up between U.S. negotiators and the Iranians but I don't think the U.S. actions are based on trust.

Mr. Kinzinger raised an important point. I had the privilege of listening to some of the investigators who tracked back not only the IEDs but it was the purchase of key electronic components for those IEDs in the United States and they were able to identify the Iranians, particularly one Iranian in Tehran, who was at the center of this network.

So I think all of them understand that we are dealing with a regime we cannot trust.

Mr. PERRY. That is exactly my point, but yet we are moving forward as if we should trust them when they have given us nothing to be trustworthy about.

Mr. ALBRIGHT. Well, I think the United States has to remain firm. I mean, I think they have conditions, they were laid out and that they should remain firm in achieving those conditions and not very much from the—I don't want to call them red lines because they tend not to use those terms but they are core—they are core requirements for a successful deal.

Mr. PERRY. Does a nuclear explosive device that—the triggering that you discussed in May, is there any other application for said device other than——

Mr. ALBRIGHT. There are always other applications, and Iran is seeking those. That is how it tries to answer this; it comes up with some civil use.

Mr. PERRY. Give us some examples, if you have them.

Mr. ALBRIGHT. Well, with the exploding bridge wires—the IAEA evidence combined on those, combined with other information is pretty clear that it was to detonate a nuclear explosive.

Iran has tried to argue no, no, it is just for other military purposes. They have tried to even concoct, I believe, some civil purposes.

You can always do that and in fact the approach Iran has taken and it could be an effective one, is to give nothing away. They deny they ever had a nuclear weapons program.

They deny the IAEA access to all information that could confirm what they are suspecting or alleging. They deny them access to facilities where they could get information and they deny them access to people.

In a sense, what Iran learned is the best lie is the total lie. So if you are going to have a front have a complete front and don't give at all. That is what, I think, Iran cannot get away with if there is going to be a deal.

Mr. PERRY. Okay. So——

Mr. POE. The gentleman's time has expired.

Mr. PERRY. Thank you, Mr. Chair.

Mr. POE. Gentleman's time has expired. I thank the gentleman. The Chair recognizes the gentleman from California, Mr. Vargas, 5 minutes.

Mr. VARGAS. And thank you, Judge Poe, and again, thank you for holding this hearing and the people who are here today testifying. I am—I think that they have denied everything and I actually never agreed to the interim agreement.

I thought it was a mistake. I continue to think it is a mistake. I think that we were naive going into this entire process. I believed that the sanctions were working.

I voted to screw down even harder sanctions and I think that that is the way we should have gone. We should have made them make that decision, do you want your nuclear program or do you want an economy—do you want a society.

Unfortunately, we didn't go down that route and here we are, and I don't believe we are going to get an agreement. I remember thinking that once we got to the end of that interim agreement that in fact it was going to be extended.

People said no, we will get to that agreement. Well, we are about to reach the extension and say well, we are going to—we are going to extend it again, and it is exactly, I think, what many of us believed.

And during the whole time they haven't stopped. They haven't gotten rid of their centrifuges. In fact, I will ask you about that. Do they still have their centrifuges? Can they still enrich? They haven't gotten rid of a single one of them, have they?

Mr. TAKEYH. They have committed to—David can speak about this—essentially transform the enriched uranium into a chemical compound that is less accessible in terms of oxidization.

Mr. VARGAS. Right. But the centrifuges themselves—have they committed to getting rid of them? Have they gotten rid of any?

Mr. TAKEYH. The parameters of the Joint Plan of Action they were not required to so. Yes.

Mr. VARGAS. That is right, and I think it has been a terrible mistake. The other thing, though, I want to—because I don't have much time, I do want to focus on the sunset because I think that is even more dangerous.

Do you remember when the revolution started there? 1979. How many years is that? Thirty-five years. Now, they want a 5-year deal. We are looking at maybe a 10- or 15- or 20-year deal, and after that they are treated the same as Japan or Germany or any of these other countries.

They get to walk out from underneath these sanctions and all these other restrictions. I mean, how can that possibly be the case?

Mr. TAKEYH. My guess would be that if there is a comprehensive plan of action negotiated it will be an extraordinary complicated document which will have stages and there will not be a single sunset clause but sunset clauses.

So some capabilities come online after 2 years, some after three, some after five and I think that is how they are going to pursue and at some end point and then the program will be unhinged from any kind of internationally mandated restrictions.

Mr. VARGAS. Would anyone else like to comment? I haven't heard that process until right now.

Mr. ALBRIGHT. Yes. Yes. I don't know the details. I mean, originally, and I heard this currently from administration officials, is they were really thinking on order of 30 years, a full generation, and that in that time they would expect Iran to have changed at least on the nuclear——

Mr. VARGAS. As they have in the last 35 years?

Mr. ALBRIGHT. Well, I am explaining on the nuclear issue. They weren't expecting them to change on the regime necessarily but on the nuclear program the people would have aged.

We saw this in the Iraqi nuclear program. I mean, the people—the nuclear experts in 2003, when I met some of them after the fall of Baghdad, were not of the caliber they had been in 1999 and 2000 when they—when they were actively engaged in their centrifuge program and in 2003 there were fewer of them.

So I think they are counting on a whole generation to have an impact. Now, the trouble is they have walked back from that 30 years and we are now hearing of 10 years, 15 years. So there will have to be some criteria on the—at the end of the deal.

It can't just be some, you know, it is tough and then suddenly it disappears. So there is going to have to be——

Mr. VARGAS. Doctor, did you have a comment on that? It seemed like you wanted to comment.

Mr. TAKEYH. Well, no. I just think that, you know, given the fact that this—I mean, I don't know the details of negotiations but given the fact that any agreement will unfold in stages, presumably at every stage Iranian nuclear capacity enlarges after the initial agreement that puts some curbs and perhaps some restrictions on it, and then the trajectory is that it will get to—it will get to a point where it is without restriction and then the decision to have an industrial-size program will be a national decision—the Iranian Government's decision and they take into account all the factors that go into that.

Mr. VARGAS. Well, I just have 20 seconds left. I guess I would say I think we are going down the wrong path. I have always believed that. I hope we get back to the sanctions and I think that they have stalled.

They have stalled magnificently. We have been caught up in it. We have been naive and we continue to be naive. Thank you, Mr. Chairman.

Mr. POE. I thank the gentleman from California. The Chair will recognize the gentleman from Arkansas, Mr. Cotton, for his 5 minutes.

Mr. COTTON. Thank you, and first, to save my time, I will associate myself with all the comments Mr. Vargas just made about the folly of pursuing this course from the outset. But here we are.

I have heard it said that any attack on a nuclear weapons system could only set back a country by 5 years because a country starting from scratch could develop nuclear weapons in 5 years with the right technical expertise.

Is that a correct estimate, in your opinions? Let me start with Mr. Albright and go down the——

Mr. ALBRIGHT. I think it is hard to know. I mean, in the case of the Iraq bombing in 1981, I mean, it may have accelerated the program. I mean, it was limping along quietly, a small program around a safeguarded reactor and after that bombing it took off.

And the issue, though, I think is—it is not—is to—if any military strategy is going to be proposed, I mean, I and my organization are opposed to those. I mean, we see it as a failure of policy.

But if anything like that was proposed, you can't go in with just one strike. I mean, you have to be able to go back. You have to ensure that any military strategy is constructed so that Iran doesn't rebuild—that it understands that to rebuild is to suffer even worse consequences.

And so that has to be more of the guiding philosophy than thinking that one strike could do much of anything.

Mr. COTTON. Mr. McInnis?

Mr. MCINNIS. What I would add, and certainly, this was, you know, something that is involved in the U.S. Central Command and other parts of the government. I think that there is, in agreement with Dr. Albright, a general understanding that you have to take, to use an Israeli expression here, mowing the lawn with this type of approach—that there is no way to really walk this all the way back more than a few years. I think this was, again, one of the reasons why, again, Iran was willing to come to the table at this stage because they had gotten this far and they don't have to go backwards or at least they could never be pushed back far enough that they couldn't recuperate. And I think that there is another, you know, issue here that, you know, that the Iranians are looking, you know, frankly, at. A potential loss of a deal, if nothing comes through in November or beyond, the prospects for a military option could be back on the table either with Israel or the U.S.

I have been, you know, in watching the Iranians talk over the last few months, you know, they have been going through some additional interesting cycles of being spooked by the Israelis and beginning in August of this year and I do think that even though I think the drop in oil prices has been a particular pressure on them this fall to make them a little bit more eager and desperate for a deal I think behind the scenes the thought that the military option may be back on the table is affecting their calculus to some degree.

Mr. COTTON. Dr. Takeyh?

Mr. TAKEYH. I agree with those statements.

Mr. COTTON. Okay. And thinking about negotiations it is always important to think about the ultimate motives or goals of your negotiating partner or adversary, as the case may be.

Thucydides said peoples go to war because of fear, interest and honor. Why do you think Iran has been pursuing a nuclear weapon for so long? Start with Dr. Takeyh and go down the other way.

Mr. TAKEYH. I do think they have a nuclear weapons program because they think that having achieved that capability, and I do think when they get to the point of threshold they will cross. I don't think they will have this sort of a murky hedge options.

It, first of all, provides them a deterrent capability and that deterrent capability gives you an ability to project power. So there is a seamless connection between projection of power and deterrence.

Mr. COTTON. Primarily against the United States and Israel?

Mr. TAKEYH. Primarily but not exclusively. So in that particular sense, also when Iran looks at the Persian Gulf the conventional balance of power tends to be—to its disfavor, given the level of Saudi armament and so on. So a combination of nuclear capability, unconventional capability married to a significant missile fleet kind of negates that.

Mr. MCINNIS. Yes. I would just add that, you know, certainly coming out of the Iran-Iraq war we knew back in the 1980s there was, you know, a real kind of prohibition, I think, in thinking about a nuclear program because the shah had pursued one.

But I think that watching what happened after the Iran-Iraq war and seeing how existential some of their crises they are facing that they would need some type of capacity to basically make us back off or make Iraq back off or, you know, or Israel or anyone else.

I mean, they look at what happened with Libya. They look at North Korea and those situations and I think they continue to take it to heart that they need something to make us never ever think about invading.

Mr. TAKEYH. If there is time I would like to have a slight disagreement with Bill but if there is not that is fine.

Mr. COTTON. It is the hands of the judge.

Mr. POE. Well, the gentleman's time has expired. Mr. Albright, you can put your answer in writing and so can you, Dr. Takeyh. The Chair will recognize the gentleman from Texas, Mr. Castro, 5 minutes.

Mr. CASTRO. Thank you, Chairman. Thank you, gentlemen, for your testimony this afternoon. I came in a little bit late so I apologize if I am retreading over ground that was covered.

But do any of you recommend an extension for the bargaining period—the negotiations period?

Mr. TAKEYH. I think November, as I mentioned, the 24th deadline is an artificial one and the administration does really have until January according to the terms of the Joint Plan of Action. So they don't really require an extension up to that point.

Mr. CASTRO. Okay.

Mr. MCINNIS. Certainly, if it actually gets us a better deal and allows some of the additional pressures to take hold, yes, I would support an extension.

Mr. ALBRIGHT. Yes. I would accept an extension. I would add, though, that it needs to be negotiated carefully because I think the current interim deal is fraying and there are problems and that those have to be addressed and so that it can't just be some simple rubber stamp extension.

Mr. CASTRO. So it sounds like the panel here is open to an extension. But let us imagine that everything falls apart and there is no agreement. What happens then?

Mr. ALBRIGHT. Well, I think—I hope and I am not encouraged, but I would hope the administration had worked up a plan of action. I mean, that is what one would expect is——

Mr. CASTRO. A plan of action on sanctions, for example?

Mr. ALBRIGHT. Well, that would include sanctions. I mean, you have to manage the escalation. Iran, in reaction to the Kirk-Menendez bill, they sent out a signal that if that bill is passed or they called it sanctions imposed that they would then start making 60 percent enriched uranium which, if you do the calculations, is awfully close to weapon grade.

Mr. CASTRO. I guess let me ask you what additional sanctions——

Mr. ALBRIGHT. You want to manage the escalation.

Mr. CASTRO. Sure, and what additional sanctions would you all impose that we aren't already doing? What are the additional sanctions you would impose?

Mr. ALBRIGHT. Well, I think Congressman Sherman had a few ideas——

Mr. CASTRO. Sure. Sure. Sure.

Mr. ALBRIGHT [continuing]. That I think there is lots of room for imposing sanctions. I think the——

Mr. CASTRO. But what specifically are the additional sanctions you would impose?

Mr. ALBRIGHT. Well, you could impose driving down the oil exports of Iran further. You could take steps to discourage any foreign companies selling to Iran. I mean, I think there is——

Mr. CASTRO. But aren't we—I mean, aren't we applying a lot of that pressure now? Are sanctions doing a lot of that now?

Mr. ALBRIGHT. No. No. There is a lot of pressure to do—there are things happening. I think another area that would be fruitfully explored is additional financial sanctions.

Not all banks are sanctioned in Iran. They have some connections to the international financial system. So I think that you could—you could explore that. I think those tend to be the most effective.

But, again, I think it—you don't want to have a wildly escalating situation.

Mr. CASTRO. Sure. Well, and let me ask you——

Mr. ALBRIGHT. Iran already knows how to make nuclear weapons.

Mr. CASTRO. Let us imagine that Iran become more isolated and the sanctions are not enough. Do you support military action against Iran?

Mr. ALBRIGHT. No, I do not.

Mr. McINNIS. Only in the most extreme circumstances where we have a clear indication that they are actually breaking out and pursuing a nuclear weapon.

Mr. CASTRO. What would that extreme circumstance look like exactly?

Mr. McINNIS. Well, it would be us detecting they actually have decided to pursue this. I think this is something that I would be very hesitant to take, given some of the implications from—it is the same reason why the Israelis have held back on the trigger for so long.

Mr. TAKEYH. And just in terms of, briefly, on the sanctions, under the previous legislation Iran, which has about five or six purchasers of oil, had to decline their oil purchases by 5 percent every several months to conform with those sanctions and not be subject to secondary measures by the United States.

Under the Joint Plan of Action, those have been suspended so the reenactment of those, I think, could affect markets. Now, whether the Chinese are going to comply to them or not I am—it is going to be difficult. As of when—I can't make that decision, Congressman, when to use military force.

I just cannot at this point have the necessary information to think about that particular issue. I think it is one of the most serious considerations that an American President has to make and he has to take into consideration a great many things before making that decision—the scope, pace of the program, the ramifications of that attack.

There is one thing and only one thing that Hitler knew and that was war—he used to say war is like stepping into a dark room—you could step on something toxic or nothing at all, but you never know until you walk in.

So you are essentially suggesting when do you walk into the dark room.

Mr. CASTRO. How much time do I have, Chair? How am I doing?

Mr. POE. Twenty seconds.

Mr. CASTRO. All right. I yield back.

Mr. POE. I thank the gentleman. I will say this to the gentleman from Arkansas who wanted to continue to ask questions, congratulations on your election and you will find that in the Senate they have no time limits on anything.

So you will be able to pontificate and ask questions indefinitely.

Mr. COTTON. I am going to have to learn to be much more long winded then.

Mr. POE. I want to thank all the gentlemen for being here. The information has been excellent. And this subcommittee is adjourned. Thank you.

[Whereupon, at 3:31 p.m., the subcommittee was adjourned.]

A P P E N D I X

SUBCOMMITTEE HEARING NOTICE
COMMITTEE ON FOREIGN AFFAIRS
U.S. HOUSE OF REPRESENTATIVES
WASHINGTON, DC 20515-6128

Subcommittee on Terrorism, Nonproliferation, and Trade

Ted Poe (R-TX), Chairman

TO: **MEMBERS OF THE COMMITTEE ON FOREIGN AFFAIRS**

You are respectfully requested to attend an OPEN hearing of the Committee on Foreign Affairs, to be held by the Subcommittee on Terrorism, Nonproliferation, and Trade in Room 2200 of the Rayburn House Office Building (and available live on the Committee website at http://www.ForeignAffairs.house.gov):

DATE: Tuesday, November 18, 2014

TIME: 2:00 p.m.

SUBJECT: Iranian Nuclear Talks: Negotiating a Bad Deal?

WITNESSES: Ray Takeyh, Ph.D.
Senior Fellow for Middle Eastern Studies
Council on Foreign Relations

Mr. J. Matthew McInnis
Resident Fellow
American Enterprise Institute

Mr. David Albright
President
Institute for Science and International Security

By Direction of the Chairman

The Committee on Foreign Affairs seeks to make its facilities accessible to persons with disabilities. If you are in need of special accommodations, please call 202/225-5021 at least four business days in advance of the event, whenever practicable. Questions with regard to special accommodations in general (including availability of Committee materials in alternative formats and assistive listening devices) may be directed to the Committee.

COMMITTEE ON FOREIGN AFFAIRS

MINUTES OF SUBCOMMITTEE ON _____ *Terrorism, Nonproliferation and Trade* _____ HEARING

Day___ *Tuesday* ___Date___ *November 18, 2014* ___Room_____ *2200* _____

Starting Time ___ *2:00 p.m.* ___ Ending Time ___ *3:31 p.m.* ___

Recesses [____] (____to ____) (____to ____) (____to ____) (____to ____) (____to ____) (____to ____)

Presiding Member(s)

Chairman Poe

Check all of the following that apply:

Open Session ☑   Electronically Recorded (taped) ☑
Executive (closed) Session ☐   Stenographic Record ☑
Televised ☑

TITLE OF HEARING:

Iranian Nuclear Talks: Negotaitaing a Bad Deal?

SUBCOMMITTEE MEMBERS PRESENT:

Reps. Poe, Wilson, Kinzinger, Brooks, Cotton, Cook, Perry, Yoho, Sherman, Lowenthal, Castro, Vargas, Schneider, Kennedy

NON-SUBCOMMITTEE MEMBERS PRESENT: *(Mark with an * if they are not members of full committee.)*

HEARING WITNESSES: Same as meeting notice attached? Yes ☑ **No** ☐
(If "no", please list below and include title, agency, department, or organization.)

STATEMENTS FOR THE RECORD: *(List any statements submitted for the record.)*

TIME SCHEDULED TO RECONVENE _____
or
TIME ADJOURNED ___ *3:31 p.m.* ___

_____
Subcommittee Staff Director